Classical Subjects *Creatively* Taught™

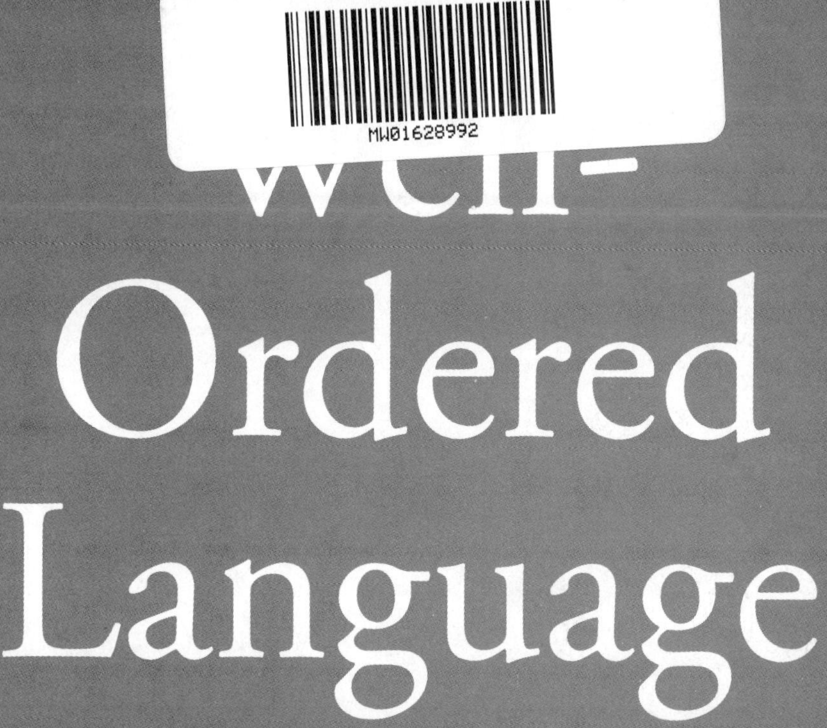

Well-Ordered Language

Level 1B

The Curious Child's Guide to Grammar

Tammy Peters and Daniel Coupland, PhD

Well-Ordered Language:
The Curious Child's Guide to Grammar
Level 1B

Version 1.0

ISBN: 978-1-60051-291-9

Classical Academic Press
515 S. 32nd St.
Camp Hill, PA 17011

www.ClassicalAcademicPress.com

Content editor: Marie Kramb Campbell, PhD
Illustrator: Katharina Drees
Series editor and book designer: Lauraine Gustafson

KP.11.22

Acknowledgments

Tammy Peters

I am deeply indebted to Mars Hill Academy in Cincinnati, Ohio. I give a sincere thanks to the students, families, and teachers who have supported me and contributed to this work over the last fifteen years. A special thanks to Sharon Peterson, Ellen Liebing, and Traci DeBra for their constant encouragement and insights, as well as to Alicia Weber, Natalie Walls, and Molly Milligan.

With a grateful heart, I thank Dr. Dan Coupland for his insights and love of language. It has been a privilege to coauthor Well-Ordered Language with him. I also thank Dr. Marie Campbell, our content editor, for her expertise and precision in the English language. She is a joy and a friend. I greatly appreciate Dr. Chris Perrin, Laurie Gustafson, and the whole Classical Academic Press staff for their vision and professionalism.

There are not enough words to express my gratitude to my family for their constant support. My heartfelt appreciation is to the love of my life, Hud Peters, who has prayerfully supported me through it all.

Daniel Coupland, PhD

I am grateful for the *grammarphiles* in my life: Mrs. Linda Tiarks, my elementary school teacher who showed me how to study and love the English language; Dr. Bryan Coupland, my father, who appreciates a well-crafted sentence; and Mrs. Tammy Peters, my coauthor, who is the most talented (and most energetic) grammar teacher I have ever seen. I am also thankful for Marie, our talented content editor, who has helped to make the Well-Ordered Language program even better. And of course, I appreciate Chris, Laurie, and the entire Classical Academic Press team for their tireless effort to get this program in print.

Well-Ordered Language Level 1

At a Glance

Book A

Chapter	Main Topic	Supplemental Topics
1	Four Kinds of Sentences	
2	Principal Elements, Part 1—Subject and Predicate	
3	Principal Elements, Part 2—Subject and Predicate Verb	Singular and plural subjects with the helping verbs *is* and *are*
4	Adverbs	*Not* and *never* as adverbs; placement of adverbs in sentence order
5	Adjectives	Correct usage of articles *a* and *an*
6	Direct Objects	Word order in sentences
7	Subject Pronouns	Agreement in number: subject pronouns and antecedents; subject pronouns and verbs
8	Interrogative Sentences—Subject Pronouns and Helping Verbs	Contractions: subject pronouns and helping verbs

Book B

Chapter	Main Topic	Supplemental Topics
1	Object Pronouns	Contractions with *not*
2	Pronoun Review	Subject/verb agreement in number and person
3	Prepositional Phrases—Adverbial	Abbreviations for months; capitalization and periods; proper and common nouns
4	Introductory Prepositional Phrases	Revising fragments
5	Compound Subjects	Subject/verb agreement with conjunctions *and*, *or*
6	Compound Verbs	Synonyms; conjunctions *and*, *or*
7	Compound Direct Objects	Word order in sentences; proper and common nouns

Table of Contents

Well-Ordered Language

A Classical Approach to English Grammar Instruction

Why Study Grammar?

We study grammar because we wish to master language, and language cannot be easily mastered without grammar. Grammar is the study of what makes language work—the way letters form words, the way words form sentences, the way sentences express human thought.

An educated person wants to understand the rich variety of human thought enshrined in language of all sorts—books from yesterday and the last millennium, books in English and books in other languages as well. An educated person also yearns to express himself clearly, accurately, and completely. It is the study of grammar that yields the capacity to do this, and the student who sees the connection between the study of grammar and the mastery of language will study grammar with zeal.

Learning Grammar, Teaching Grammar

We have designed Well-Ordered Language (WOL) with the understanding that many teachers who will use this book don't know grammar as well as they would like. As a result, we have created a rich teacher's edition that will enable teachers to review and deepen their own understanding of grammar even as they teach students.

We have also worked to provide a clear, incremental presentation of grammar in this series that includes plenty of illustrations, practice, and review. For example, in each chapter, students will memorize through song clear definitions of relevant grammatical concepts. Helpful analogies and attractive graphical illustrations at the beginning of each chapter introduce and complement the concepts in the chapter. Students also will discover emerging from the sentence exercises a story that features characters who appear throughout the text and in the graphical illustrations.

Effective Teaching Methods

The series employs an innovative choral analysis method that makes learning enjoyable and permanent. With clear guidance from the teacher's edition, instructors will easily be able to lead students through the choral analysis of grammar, and through this analysis, students will see grammar embodied in the sentences they study. The program has been layered concept on concept, an approach that aids students in seeing and experiencing how a well-ordered language works and how it increases their understanding and enjoyment of literature, stories, and poetry.

Learning with Delight

We think that the right study of grammar should lead to delight. The traditional study of grammar should be more than mere rote memorization of rules; it must also include opportunities for students to engage language in works of literature and human expression. As students acquire a greater capacity to understand language and use it effectively themselves, they will experience joy and delight. This is one reason we have included for grammatical study beautiful poetry and excerpts from great literature. Students will see that their ongoing study of grammar will open up a deeper understanding of beautiful literature that both instructs and delights.

Compelling Need

In this cultural moment, there is a desperate need for language that is well ordered. Today's discourse is often filled with ambiguity, equivocation, and crudeness. Those who have mastered a well-ordered language not only will stand out as eloquent and clear but also will be able to say well what they mean and to say what others will heed. It will be those with a command of language who will be able to mine the wisdom of the past and to produce eloquence in the future.

Ongoing Support

We have created not only a series of texts but a constellation of products that will help teachers to use WOL effectively. Visit our website at ClassicalAcademicPress.com for additional support for using WOL, including video training (featuring author Tammy Peters), downloadable PDF documents, and other resources.

Thank you for joining us in this most important work of restoring a well-ordered language for the next generation!

Lesson-Planning Options

The Well-Ordered Language series is designed to be flexible, adaptable, and practical. Depending on her needs, the teacher can modify lessons to meet particular classroom expectations. The following options for teaching each chapter assume a 30–40 minute period.

	Option A (4 times per week)	Option B (3 times per week)	Option C (5 times, one week)
Week One	**Day One** ◇ Chapter Introduction ◇ Introductory Lesson ◇ Introductory Practice	**Day One** ◇ Chapter Introduction ◇ Introductory Lesson ◇ Introductory Practice	**Day One** ◇ Chapter Introduction ◇ Introductory Lesson ◇ Introductory Practice
	Day Two ◇ Lessons to Learn A ◇ Lessons to Practice A	**Day Two** ◇ Lessons to Learn A ◇ Lessons to Practice A	**Day Two** ◇ Lessons to Learn A ◇ Lessons to Practice A
	Day Three ◇ Lessons to Learn B ◇ Lessons to Practice B	**Day Three** ◇ Lessons to Learn B ◇ Lessons to Practice B	**Day Three** ◇ Lessons to Learn B ◇ Lessons to Practice B
	Day Four ◇ Fable* ◇ Fable Sentences (PDF)		**Day Four** ◇ Lessons to Learn C ◇ Lessons to Practice C
			Day Five ◇ Quiz (PDF)
Week Two	**Day Five** ◇ Lessons to Learn C ◇ Lessons to Practice C	**Day Four** ◇ Lessons to Learn C ◇ Lessons to Practice C ***or*** ◇ Lessons to Learn—Review ◇ Lessons to Practice—Review	
	Day Six ◇ Lessons to Learn—Review ◇ Lessons to Practice—Review	**Day Five** ◇ Lessons to Learn—Review ◇ Lessons to Practice—Review ***or*** ◇ Fable*/Fable Sentences (PDF)	
	Day Seven ◇ Poem*/Poem Activity ***or*** ◇ Practice Sheet (PDF)	**Day Six** ◇ Quiz (PDF)	
	Day Eight ◇ Quiz (PDF)		

*The fables for chapters 1, 3, 5, 6, 7, and 8 can be found in the downloadable PDF. The poems for chapters 2 and 4 can be found in the PDF.

Introduction to Students

Do you have a favorite word? Most people have favorite words just as they have favorite numbers or colors. So, what is yours?

Maybe it is an exceedingly (very) long word that your friends don't know. Maybe you just like the way its sound rolls off your tongue. Maybe you use it as often as you can, or maybe you save it for special occasions.

We want to share one of our favorite words with you. You probably know what it means already, but you may not have thought of it as an exceptional word. Probably few people would name it as a favorite because it seems so ordinary. It is far from ordinary though. The word is . . . *analyze.*

One reason we love the word *analyze* is because it has interesting grandparents. Its roots are Greek: *ana* meaning "up, throughout" and *lusis* meaning "unloose, release, set free." When you *analyze* something, you break it up into its parts and set them free!

Great thinkers are great analyzers.

Scientists who study bugs are called entomologists. They analyze insects by dissecting them. Sports analysts watch freeze frames of each motion of a single play in football to make sure the referee applied the rules correctly. Detectives analyze every inch of a crime scene, inspecting it for clues. These great thinkers are curious about what is inside an insect, a play, or even a crime.

Great thinkers are always curious. For them, analysis is an adventure.

You are a curious child, and your adventure in this book will be learning how to *analyze* sentences. You will take them apart, unloose their knots, and dissect them. Step by step you will learn the special function of each part of language.

Understanding the parts of something—whether you are a student, scientist, sports analyst, or detective—leads to appreciating the whole thing even more. Once you break something apart, it is natural and right that you should put it back together again. If you take apart a clock to see how it works, you will want to reassemble it so you don't miss dinnertime. Learning how to *analyze* sentences makes you more skilled at *constructing* them too, both in your writing and in your speaking.

The parts of language are words, and words are wonderful.

Chapter 1

Object Pronouns

Sometimes teachers need substitutes. Have you ever come to school and discovered your teacher was sick and someone else was standing in for her? You know that the substitute is not your "real" teacher, but you also know that he replaces your teacher and has the authority to teach the class. He is acting in her absence. He takes her place. Having a substitute teacher can be an interesting change from the way things are usually done in your classroom, but for the most part it makes little difference whether your teacher is the regular one or a substitute. They both do the same work in the classroom, and they follow the same rules.

Sometimes substitutes are needed when baking. What if you were baking your favorite treat—chocolate chip cookies—to share at school on your birthday, but one of your friends really doesn't like chocolate? In some of the cookies, you could substitute raisins for chocolate chips. All the treats on the serving plate are still cookies, but there is an assortment, or variety, to choose from. Similarly, when you substitute pronouns for nouns, you add variety to your sentences.

Pronouns■ in a sentence are like substitute teachers in a classroom or substitute ingredients in a recipe—they can replace, or stand in for something. They are used to replace, or stand in for, nouns. Pronouns follow the same rules and behave just like nouns whether they are subjects or direct objects. Like substitute teachers in the classroom, pronouns do the same work in the sentence as the nouns they replace. Like raisins in a chocolate chip cookie recipe, pronouns also add a little variety to sentences.

To the Source:

■ pronoun

The word *pronoun* comes from the Latin word *pronomen,* which literally means "in place of a noun." *Pro* means "in place of" and *nomen* means "name" or "noun."

Off the Shelf: Even if you have already read E.B. White's popular novel *Charlotte's Web*, you'll enjoy reading it again. We can learn a lot from this barnyard society, especially from a clever, caring spider who "spins" a plot to save the life of a beloved pig. Do you remember the colorful character Templeton, the selfish barn rat? Read the longer passage from chapter 6 of *Charlotte's Web* in The Curious Child's Literary Appendix or check out the book at your library.

Ideas to Understand

There are several types of pronouns, all of which are used in place of nouns. You have already learned about personal subject pronouns (see *WOL1A* chapter 7). You've also heard of the type of pronoun we're going to focus on in this chapter: the object pronoun. An object pronoun is a personal pronoun that is used in the place of a direct object (or **object of the preposition**).

In the novel *Charlotte's Web*, E.B. White uses the object pronoun *it* in place of the word egg when the rat, Templeton, asks for the goose and gander's (male goose) extra "dud" egg:

> "What are you going to do with it?" continued Templeton, his little round beady eyes fixed on the goose.
> "You can have it," replied the goose. "Roll it away and add it to that nasty collection of yours."[1]

Templeton's question, "What are you going to do with it?" includes the object pronoun *it* as the object of the preposition *with*. (*With it* is a prepositional phrase. You will learn about prepositional phrases in chapter 3.) The goose's answer, "You can have it," uses the object pronoun *it* as the direct object. The goose's next sentence (which is an imperative sentence, by the way) also uses *it* twice as a direct object—*roll it* and *add it*. E.B. White uses pronouns to help his story flow better. (You learned about how pronouns help the flow of a sentence or story in chapter 7 of *WOL1A*.) Without pronouns, the sentences would be choppy: *What are you going to do with **the egg**? You can have **the egg**. Roll **the egg** away and add **the egg** to that nasty collection.* That's too many eggs!

Do you remember how pronouns are classified? We classify them according to how they function in a sentence. So, an object pronoun functions as either a direct object or an object of the preposition. We also classify pronouns according to their person (first, second, or third) and number (singular or plural). The following chart will help you understand how object pronouns are organized:

1. E.B. White, "Summer Days," *Charlotte's Web* (New York: HarperTrophy, 1980), pp. 45–46.

Object Pronouns

	Singular	Plural
First Person	me	us
Second Person	you	you
Third Person	him, her, it	them

Terms to Remember

It is very important to memorize the object pronouns and be able to distinguish them from the subject pronouns. By doing so, you can avoid the many grammatical mistakes that happen when speakers or writers use an object pronoun when they should use a subject pronoun and vice versa. Just as distinguishing an insect from a spider is a very basic and necessary skill in entomology (the study of insects), so is distinguishing the different kinds of pronouns in sentence analysis.

Pronoun *(1–11)*

A pronoun is a part of speech
  used in place of a noun or nouns.
A pronoun is a part of speech
  used in place of a noun or nouns.
A pronoun is a part of speech.

Subject Pronouns *(1–12)*

Subject pronouns are in the nominative case:
  I, you, he, she, it, we, you, they *(repeat).*
Subject pronouns are in the nominative case:
  I, you, he, she, it, we, you, they *(repeat).*

Antecedents *(1–13)*

The antecedent is a noun, clause, or phrase
  to which a pronoun refers.
If the antecedent is singular,
  then the pronoun is singular too.

But if the noun, clause, or phrase is plural,
then the pronoun must be plural too.
The antecedent determines which pronoun is used.

NEW! **Object Pronouns** *(1–15)*

Object pronouns are in the objective case.
Me, you, him, her, it, us, you, them
Me, you, him, her, it, us, you, them.
Object pronouns are in the objective case.
Me, you, him, her, it, us, you, them
Me, you, him, her, it, us, you, them
Me, you, him, her, it, us, you, them.

A Sentence to Analyze

Now it's time to include object pronouns in sentence analysis. As with subject pronouns, object pronouns are easy to analyze because they behave like nouns. You didn't forget how to analyze sentences, did you?

With your teacher's guidance, use the following steps to analyze the sentence. Speak the words in gray along with your teacher and pay close attention to what she is writing. When your teacher is finished, the sentence will look like this:

S PV
Templeton wants it.
do

a. First, read the sentence aloud. "Templeton wants it."

b. "This is a sentence and it is declarative."

c. "This sentence is about *Templeton*. So, Templeton is the subject because it is what the sentence is about." (Since *Templeton* is the subject, underline it and place a capital letter *S* above it.)

d. "This sentence tells us that Templeton *wants*. So, *wants* is the predicate because it is what the sentence tells us about *Templeton*." (Since *wants* tells something about Templeton, double underline it and place a capital letter *P* above it.) "It is a predicate verb because it shows action. There is no linking verb because predicate verbs do not need linking verbs." (Since *wants* shows action, place a capital letter *V* to the right of the letter *P* above the predicate.)

e. "*It* tells us what Templeton wants." (Since *it* tells us what Templeton wants, draw a circle around it.)

f. "So, *it* is an objective element because it completes the meaning of an action verb. It is a direct object because it tells what Templeton wants." (Write *do* in lowercase letters beneath the direct object.)

Even if you love chocolate chip cookies, raisin cookies do the trick when you want something sweet and need to replace the chocolate. Even if you really like your teacher, you probably welcome having substitutes sometimes. They bring variety to a school day, and they make sure you don't miss anything important in the absence of your teacher. Even when you use a great noun, you may need to replace it with an object pronoun in the next sentence. Object pronouns don't just stand in for nouns. They also get rid of unnecessary repetition. Sentences flow more smoothly and with more variety when object pronouns fill in for nouns as direct objects or objects of prepositions.

Do you remember the Clark family: Mom, Dad, Winston, Heidi, Fritz, and their mischievous dog, Rex? What about their cousins—Theo, Peggy, and Lucy—and the rest of the extended family—Aunt Gabby, Uncle Ulysses, Grandma, and Grandpa? In the sentences you'll be studying throughout this book, you'll continue reading about some of their adventures as a family.

Study the illustration at the beginning of this chapter. How many cookies, baked and unbaked, can you see? How many dozen is that? Do you think Rex should get one too?

Review It

Can you define the following five grammar terms from memory?

Direct objects

Antecedents

Object pronouns

Pronouns

Subject pronouns

Learn It

Do you remember what contractions are? Contractions are abbreviated words created by eliminating letters (sounds) and inserting apostrophes in their places. You probably also remember that in addition to making contractions with subject pronouns and verbs such as *is*, *are*, *will*, *would*, *have*, *has*, and *had*, we can make contractions with verbs and the adverb *not*. When you form a contraction with the adverb *not*, it makes the original meaning of a verb negative. We form the contraction by deleting the space between the verb and *not* and replacing the *o* in *not* with an apostrophe. The word *cannot* is unusual because the verb and *not* are already one word, so the apostrophe replaces one *n* and the *o* like this: *can't*. The contraction for *will not* is also irregular: *won't*.

On the blanks provided, write the contractions for the following words.

Example: *is not* = isn't

1. do not ______________________________
2. does not ______________________________
3. did not ______________________________
4. cannot ______________________________

5. could not ______________________________

6. should not ______________________________

7. will not ______________________________

8. must not ______________________________

Analyze It

Analyze the following sentences (*S* = subject; *PV* = predicate verb; *hv* = helping verb; *adv* = adverb; *adj* = adjective; *do* = direct object).

1. Uncle Ulysses will not read it tonight.

2. Earlier the little cousins read it together.

Introductory Practice
Object Pronouns

1. Analyze the following sentences (*S* = subject; *PV* = predicate verb; *hv* = helping verb; *adv* = adverb; *adj* = adjective; *do* = direct object).

   a. The cold winter winds blew it away.

   b. The slushy sleet covered them.

   c. Will Winston chase it now?

   d. Suddenly Grandpa calls us back.

2. Fill in the following chart with the correct object pronouns.

Object Pronouns

	Singular	Plural
First Person	__________	__________
Second Person	__________	__________
Third Person	__________	__________

3. Remember, contractions are shortened versions of words created by taking out letters (sounds) and inserting apostrophes (') in their places. On the blanks provided, write the contractions for the following words.

   a. did not ______________________________

   b. must not ______________________________

   c. cannot ______________________________

   d. should not ______________________________

   e. do not ______________________________

   f. might not ______________________________

Lessons to Learn

Object Pronouns

Review It

As you learned in *WOL1A*, mastering definitions requires reviewing them often.

List the eight subject pronouns.

List the eight object pronouns.

Which pronouns are singular?

Which pronouns are plural?

Learn It

Listen while your teacher directs you to fill in the following object pronoun chart.

Example:

Teacher: "Please fill in the first-person plural object pronoun."
Students write *us* in the correct space on the chart.

	Singular	Plural
First Person	me	us
Second Person	you	you
Third Person	him, her, it	them

Lessons to Learn
Object Pronouns

Analyze It

1. Grandma warmly greeted her.

2. Grandpa lifted her high too.

Lessons to Practice

Object Pronouns

1. Analyze the following sentences (*S* = subject; *PV* = predicate verb; *hv* = helping verb; *adv* = adverb; *adj* = adjective; *do* = direct object).

   a. The neighbors were watching us carefully.

   b. I should have been carrying it correctly.

   c. Dad showed me again.

   d. Do you always haul them separately?

2. Fill in the following chart with the correct object pronouns.

Object Pronouns

	Singular	Plural
First Person		
Second Person		
Third Person		

3. Fill in the blanks with the two words that make up each of the following contractions. (Hint: There are two contractions in this list that could be split into two different sets of words.)

a. it's ______________________

b. we're ______________________

c. I'm ______________________

d. he's ______________________

e. they're ______________________

f. you're ______________________

Lessons to Learn
Object Pronouns

Review it

Answers the following review questions.

What is a verb?

What are the four classes of verbs?

What is an intransitive verb?

What is a direct object?

What is a transitive verb?

What is a helping verb?

Learn It

Pronouns behave like the nouns they represent. In the following sentences, underline the noun that is behaving like a direct object and then rewrite the sentence with the correct object pronoun. Keep on your toes! Notice how the article, and sometimes the adjective, is replaced along with the direct object when an object pronoun is substituted.

Example: Fritz spotted some <u>bats</u>. **Fritz spotted *them*.**

1. Aunt Gabby saw the sunset. Aunt Gabby saw it
2. The sky displayed rosy clouds. The sky displayed them
3. Dad brought Winston and me along. Dad brought him and me along
4. Fritz spotted a meteorite. fritZ Spotted it

meteorite: a rock or pieces of rock that fall from an asteroid or comet and reaches the surface of the earth

5. Rex just watched Fritz. Rex just watched
him

Analyze It

Analyze the following sentences (*S* = subject; *PV* = predicate verb; *hv* = helping verb; *adv* = adverb; *adj* = adjective; *do* = direct object).

1. Unfortunately the baseball hit him yesterday.

2. The whole team discussed it together.

Lessons to Practice
Object Pronouns

1. Analyze the following sentences (*S* = subject; *PV* = predicate verb; *hv* = helping verb; *adv* = adverb; *adj* = adjective; *do* = direct object).

   a. The vessel should have brought us too.

   b. Suddenly the sailor spotted him.

   c. The whale might accidentally spray them.

   d. Will you snap it quickly?

2. Fill in the following chart with the correct object pronouns.

Object Pronouns

	Singular	Plural
First Person		
Second Person		
Third Person		

3. Fill in the blanks with the two words that make up each of the following contractions.

   a. haven't have not

   b. won't will not

   c. isn't is not

   d. aren't are not

   e. hadn't had not

   f. weren't were not

Review It

Grammar terms are the building blocks of learning. Have you memorized the answers to the following questions yet?

What is a pronoun?

What are the subject pronouns?

What are the object pronouns?

What is an antecedent?

Learn It

As you know, contractions are two words shortened into a single word by taking out letters (sounds) and inserting apostrophes (') in their places. When you form a contraction with the adverb *not*, it makes the original meaning of a verb negative. Fill in the blanks with the two words that make up each of the following contractions.

Example: isn't = is not

1. aren't are not
2. wasn't was not
3. weren't were not
4. haven't have not
5. hadn't had not
6. hasn't has not
7. won't will not
8. wouldn't would not

Lessons to Learn
Object Pronouns

Analyze It

Analyze the following sentences (*S* = subject; *PV* = predicate verb; *hv* = helping verb; *adv* = adverb; *adj* = adjective; *do* = direct object).

1. Did the children find him afterward?

2. Curiously Winston asked them again.

Lessons to Practice

Object Pronouns

1. Analyze the following sentences (*S* = subject; *PV* = predicate verb; *hv* = helping verb; *adv* = adverb; *adj* = adjective; *do* = direct object).

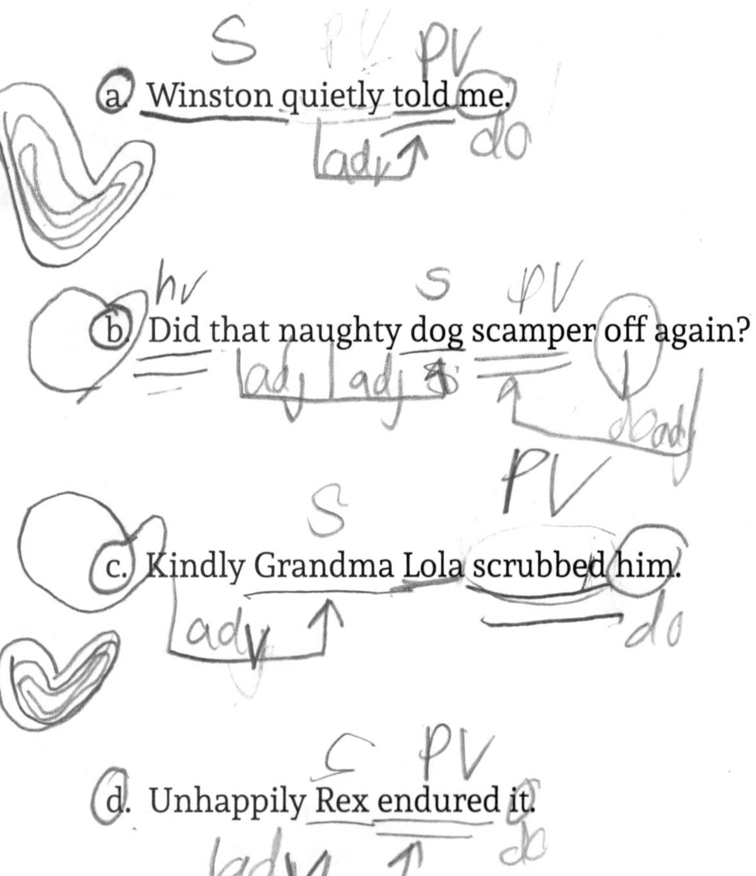

a. Winston quietly told me.

b. Did that naughty dog scamper off again?

c. Kindly Grandma Lola scrubbed him.

d. Unhappily Rex endured it.

2. Fill in the following chart with the correct object pronouns.

Object Pronouns

	Singular	Plural
First Person	we	us
Second Person	you	you
Third Person	him her it	them

3. Fill in the blanks with the two words that make up each of the following contractions.

   a. didn't did not
   b. shouldn't should not
   c. can't cannot
   d. mustn't must not
   e. don't do not
   f. mightn't might not

Review It

How good is your memory? Let's test it!

What is a direct object? Think of a sentence with a direct object.

What is a pronoun?

What is an antecedent?

List eight subject pronouns.

List eight object pronouns.

Learn It

Construct sentences using the following transitive verbs and object pronouns. Remember, a transitive verb is a verb that takes an objective element.

Example:

Verb: catch
Pronoun: him
Sentence: Fritz will *catch him*.

Verbs	Object Pronouns
catch(es)	me
help(s)	you
gather(s)	him
knead(s)	her
swat(s)	it
scratch(es)	us
follow(s)	you
choose(s)	them

Verbs	Object Pronouns
share(s)	
change(s)	
write(s)	
wash(es)	
doubt(s)	

1. ______________________________

____

2. ______________________________

____

3. ______________________________

____

4. ______________________________

____

5. ______________________________

____

Lessons to Practice—Review
Object Pronouns

1. Analyze the following sentences (*S* = subject; *PV* = predicate verb; *hv* = helping verb; *adv* = adverb; *adj* = adjective; *do* = direct object).

   a. Does the coach drill them regularly?

   b. Coach Howard is now calling her over.

   c. The grateful player regarded him respectfully.

   d. Playfully the team threw it high.

2. Fill in the following chart with the correct object pronouns.

Object Pronouns

	Singular	Plural
First Person	________________	________________
Second Person	________________	________________
Third Person	________________	________________

3. Fill in the blanks with the two words that make up each of the following contractions. (Hint: There is one contraction in this list that could be split into two different sets of words.)

   a. you're ______________________________

   b. doesn't ______________________________

   c. they're ______________________________

   d. she's ______________________________

   e. hadn't ______________________________

   f. can't ______________________________

Lessons to Enjoy—Fable
Object Pronouns

Sometimes the solution to a problem may not be as easy as it seems. In this fable, a large family of mice must solve a problem with a pesky cat. Read to find out how the impossible task is to be performed and by whom.

The Mice in Council

by Aesop

dread: fear

fearsome: causing fear

bell (verb): to put a bell on

Something had to be done about the Cat! Hardly a day went by that the Mice didn't hear of some brother or sister, aunt or uncle, having gotten gobbled down by the Cat. The Mice lived in such constant dread of her claws that they hardly dared to stir from their dens by night or day. Finally they called a meeting to decide on a plan to free themselves from their fearsome enemy.

Many plans were discussed, but none of them sounded good enough. At last, a very Young Mouse got up and said, "I have a plan that seems very simple, but I know it will be successful. All we have to do is to hang a bell about the Cat's neck. When we hear the bell ringing, we will know immediately that our enemy is coming."

All the Mice were much surprised that they had not thought of such a plan before. "Hurrah for the Young Mouse!" they shouted.

As they were cheering and rejoicing over their good fortune, an Old Mouse stood up. Shaking a finger at the gathering, he said, "I will say that the plan of the Young Mouse is very good. But let me ask one question: Who will bell the Cat?"

Moral: It is one thing to say that something should be done, but quite a different matter to do it.[1]

1. Aesop, "The Mice in Council," in *Writing & Rhetoric Book 1: Fable*, by Paul Kortepeter (Camp Hill, PA: Classical Academic Press, 2013), p. 60.

Questions to Ponder

1. What do the Mice want?
2. What does it mean to live in "constant dread"?
3. How would you put in your own words what the wise old Mouse says at the end of the fable?
4. What does the old Mouse's statement have to do with the moral of the fable?

Chapter 2

Pronoun Review

In your house you probably have a kitchen drawer where your parents keep all sorts of utensils, such as spatulas, whisks, a corkscrew, a rolling pin, and other interesting gadgets. Each kitchen tool has a different job. You wouldn't whisk eggs with a spatula, stir soup with a corkscrew, or flip a pancake with a rolling pin. Knowing to use the right tool for the right job just makes sense.

Pronouns are like tools you can pull out of your grammar gadget drawer to help you whip up an interesting sentence. You have already learned what the different pronouns are—which ones are subject pronouns and which ones are object pronouns—and how they stand in for specific nouns in a sentence. Now it is time to practice choosing the right pronoun tool for the right job in a sentence. For instance, when you use a subject pronoun, it determines whether the verb in the sentence is singular or plural. Then, another thing to consider is that placing a subject pronoun between the helping verb and the main verb signals that the sentence is interrogative. Finally, some pronouns can be used only as objects, and it's important not to confuse them with subject pronouns.

There are many types of pronouns, just as there are many tools in a kitchen. In this chapter we are reviewing subject pronouns and object pronouns. All this may sound tricky, but you are becoming more and more skilled in the grammar kitchen. Let's open our gadget drawer, review the personal pronouns, and see what we can create!

Off the Shelf: Rudyard Kipling's *Just So Stories* are called *pourquoi* stories. *Pourquoi* is the French word for *why*. These stories are fanciful tales of *why* certain animals have trunks or humps or spots or other characteristics shared only by their own species (kind). "The Beginning of the Armadillos" tells the story of how the turtle and the hedgehog transformed into the first armadillo. You can find a longer passage of the story in The Curious Child's Literary Appendix. Do you want to read the whole story? Take it off the shelf and check it out at your library.

Ideas to Understand

The first tools to take out of the drawer are the subject pronouns. Pronouns enable the speaker or writer to communicate meaning without using the nouns over and over again. In the tale "The Beginning of the Armadillos" from *Just So Stories*, author Rudyard Kipling tells about a conversation between a tortoise and a small jaguar cub named Painted Jaguar. The tortoise, named Slow-and-Solid, is discussing with Painted Jaguar what the cub's mother had told him earlier about how to eat a tortoise. Slow-and-Solid shrewdly relies on pronouns to trick Painted Jaguar into forgetting his mother's instructions:

> Well, suppose you say that I said that she said something quite different, I don't see that it makes any difference; because if she said what you said I said she said, it's just the same as if I said what she said she said.[1]

This passage is meant to be light and humorous. Slow-and-Solid is trying to confuse Painted Jaguar. Let's replace the pronouns with their proper noun antecedents to test whether the tortoise got them all right:

> Well, suppose *Painted Jaguar* says that *Slow-and-Solid* said that *Mother Painted Jaguar* said something quite different, *Slow-and-Solid* doesn't see that it makes any difference; because if *Mother Painted Jaguar* said what *Painted Jaguar* said *Slow-and-Solid* said *Mother Painted Jaguar* said, it's just the same as if *Slow-and-Solid* said what *Mother Painted Jaguar* said *Mother Painted Jaguar* said.

He did it! Such repetition of pronouns makes the text awkward and very confusing, but that is Kipling's joke. Nonetheless, he cleverly and correctly uses the subject pronouns *I*, *you*, and *she* to replace a proper noun as the subject of a verb.

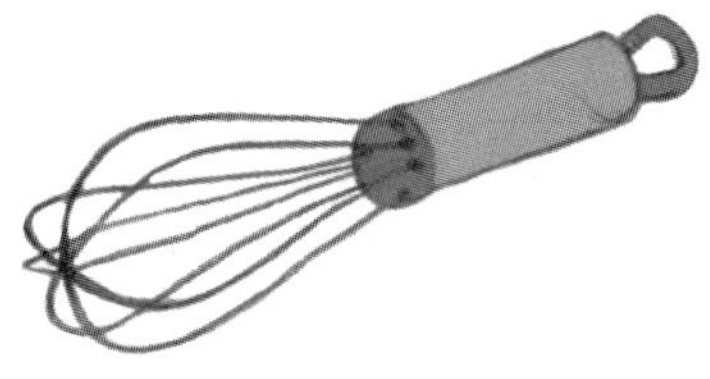

1. Rudyard Kipling, "The Beginning of the Armadillos," *Just So Stories* (New York: Doubleday, 1952), p. 39.

Subject Pronouns

	Singular	Plural
First Person	I	we
Second Person	you	you
Third Person	he, she, it	they

Now, back to the kitchen. The "recipe" for a correct sentence using pronouns demands that you choose a verb that agrees in number and in person with the subject pronoun. This is called **subject-verb agreement**. If the pronoun is singular, then the verb must be singular; if the pronoun is plural, then the verb must be plural. Depending on the person of the pronoun, the verb may change form too. Notice in the examples below how the pronouns *I*, *you*, *we*, and *they* use the same verb—*say*—while the third-person singular pronouns *he*, *she*, and *it* use a slightly different form of the verb—*says*.

	Singular	Plural
First Person	I *say* it.	We *say* it.
Second Person	You *say* it.	You *say* it.
Third Person	He ***says*** it./She ***says*** it./It ***says*** it.	They *say* it.

While we are talking about subject pronouns, and comparing them to kitchen gadgets, do you remember that there is a special "recipe" for an interrogative sentence with a subject pronoun? This recipe calls for the subject pronoun to come between the helping verb and the main verb. This order signals that the sentence is a question before you even see the question mark. *Do* (helping verb) *you* (subject pronoun) *remember* (main verb)?

The next set of gadgets in our grammar gadget drawer is our collection of object pronouns. After Slow-and-Solid tricks Painted Jaguar into releasing him into the water, Slow-and-Solid tells his prickly hedgehog friend what happened. Notice Kipling's object pronouns in this passage, which we have put in *italics*:

> I told *him* truthfully that I was a truthful Tortoise, but he wouldn't believe *it*, and he made *me* jump into the river to see if I was, and I was, and he is surprised. Now he's gone to tell his Mummy. Listen to *him*!

Here Kipling chooses only object pronouns for the objects in the sentences. If the recipe is to turn out right, object pronouns must be used as objects and subject pronouns must be used as subjects. It would be nonsense for Kipling to have written "I told he" and "listen to he" because he would have chosen subject pronouns for a direct object and an object of a preposition.

Object Pronouns

	Singular	Plural
First Person	me	us
Second Person	you	you
Third Person	him, her, it	them

Terms to Remember

When people make mistakes in grammar, the problem is often their choice of pronouns. This is why it is important to review the basic tools of grammar.

Eight Parts of Speech *(1–1)*

The eight parts of speech are classes of words
with the same kind of meaning and use.
They are: nouns, verbs, adjectives, adverbs,
prepositions, pronouns, conjunctions, interjections.
These are the eight parts of speech,
classes of words with the same kind of meaning and use. *(Repeat.)*

Sentence *(1–2)*

A sentence is a group of words expressing a complete thought.
There are four kinds of sentences:
Declarative sentence—makes a statement.
Interrogative sentence—asks a question.
Imperative sentence—gives a command.
Exclamatory sentence—expresses strong feelings.

A sentence is a group of words expressing a complete thought.
There are four kinds of sentences. *(Repeat.)*

Principal Elements *(1–3)*

Principal elements are the parts of the sentence
that are needed for the sentence to be completed.
Subject and predicate are those two parts.

Subject Pronouns *(1–12)*

Subject pronouns are in the nominative case:
I, you, he, she, it, we, you, they *(repeat)*.
Subject pronouns are in the nominative case:
I, you, he, she, it, we, you, they *(repeat)*.

Object Pronouns *(1–15)*

Object pronouns are in the objective case.
Me, you, him, her, it, us, you, them
Me, you, him, her, it, us, you, them.
Object pronouns are in the objective case.
Me, you, him, her, it, us, you, them
Me, you, him, her, it, us, you, them
Me, you, him, her, it, us, you, them.

A Sentence to Analyze

Remember to say the analysis aloud, with expression, while you mark the sentence neatly.

S PV
We saw her
do

we saw her

a. (First, read the sentence aloud.) "We saw her."

b. "This is a sentence and it is declarative."

c. "This sentence is about *we*. So, *we* is the subject because it is what the sentence is about." (Since *we* is the subject, underline it and place a capital letter *S* above it.)

d. "This sentence tells us that we *saw*. So, *saw* is the predicate because it is what the sentence tells us about *we*." (Since *saw* tells us something about *we*, double underline it and place a capital letter *P* above it.) "It is a predicate verb because it shows action. There is no linking verb because predicate verbs do not need linking verbs." (Since *saw* shows action, place a capital letter *V* to the right of the letter *P* above the predicate.)

e. "*Her* tells us what we saw." (Since *her* tells what we saw, draw a circle around *her*.)

f. "So, *her* is an objective element because it completes the meaning of an action verb. It is a direct object because it tells *what* we saw." (Write *do* in lowercase letters beneath the direct object.)

Usually your ear naturally distinguishes between pronouns, and you choose correctly between subject and object pronouns and between singular and plural verbs. But when you start writing more complicated sentences, just like a chef creating more complicated recipes, you will be glad that you have memorized and analyzed the basic ingredients and that you have practiced choosing the best sentence tools.

Notes

Introductory Lesson
Pronoun Review

Review It

What are the definitions of the following terms?

Eight parts of speech

Sentence

Principal Elements

Subject pronouns

Object pronouns

Learn It

Although subject pronouns and object pronouns are both personal pronouns, they have different roles in a sentence. Subject pronouns can replace subject nouns, while object pronouns can replace direct objects.

In the following sentences, circle the correct pronoun.

Example: Did (we / us) bring the picnic basket?

1. (She / Her) sang the songs softly.
2. The tender mother returned (he / him) gently.
3. Unfortunately (they / them) slammed the door.
4. (He / Him) suddenly woke up.

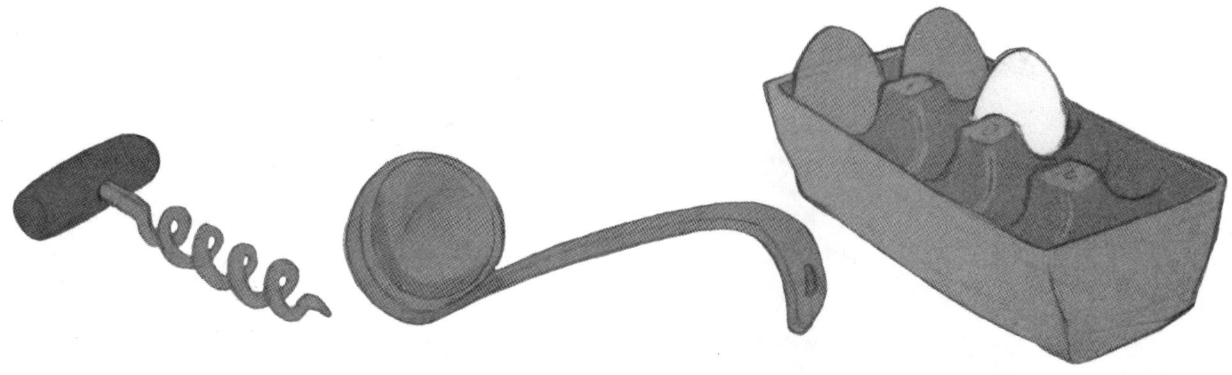

Analyze It

Analyze the following sentences (*S* = subject; *PV* = predicate verb; *hv* = helping verb; *adv* = adverb; *adj* = adjective; *do* = direct object).

1. Did you want them now?

2. Carefully she carried it alone.

Introductory Practice
Pronoun Review

1. Analyze the following sentences (*S* = subject; *PV* = predicate verb; *hv* = helping verb; *adv* = adverb; *adj* = adjective; *do* = direct object).

   a. They brought them over yesterday.

   b. He usually helps her.

   c. Next we were building it.

   d. Will you help us later?

2. What is a *pronoun*? ____

   ____

3. In the following sentences, circle the correct pronoun.

   a. The neighbors heard (I / me).

   b. Later (we / us) filled wicker baskets.

   c. Will (your / you) help afterward?

   d. (Her / She) will cut all the tree branches.

4. Imagine that Heidi and Fritz are in the garage and Heidi is trying to help Fritz get his bike helmet adjusted to fit properly. Then write a sentence about the two of them using both a *subject pronoun* and an *object pronoun.*

____

____

Lessons to Learn
Pronoun Review

Review It

Can you list the eight subject pronouns from memory? Which ones are singular? Which ones are plural? Can you list the eight object pronouns? Which ones are singular? Which ones are plural?

Learn It

1. In the following pairs of sentences, fill in the missing pronouns. Each pronoun should replace the noun antecedent that is in the first sentence in each pair.

Example: Sunflower seeds covered the ground. The cardinals ate __them__.

   a. The two sparrows flew down. We fed ____________________.

   b. I watched a blue jay. ____________________ attacked the others.

   c. The birds flew upward. Theo chased ____________________.

   d. Lucy flapped her arms. ____________________ chased the blue jay away.

   e. Grandpa threw more seeds. ____________________ blanketed the ground.

2. To continue the story of the sparrows and the blue jay, construct two sentences. Be sure to include both a subject pronoun and an object pronoun.

____

____

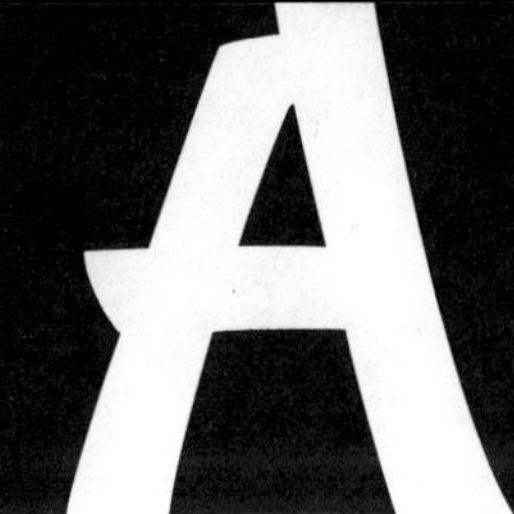

Analyze It

Analyze the following sentences (*S* = subject; *PV* = predicate verb; *hv* = helping verb; *adv* = adverb; *adj* = adjective; *do* = direct object).

1. They might not show him later.

2. Will he tell us soon?

Lessons to Practice

Pronoun Review

1. Analyze the following sentences (*S* = subject; *PV* = predicate verb; *hv* = helping verb; *adv* = adverb; *adj* = adjective; *do* = direct object).

   a. Gently he carted them back.

   b. We cheered her along too.

   c. Have you carried it before?

   d. I will not run that obstacle course again.

2. Fill in the following chart with the correct object pronouns.

Object Pronouns

	Singular	Plural
First Person	____________	____________
Second Person	____________	____________
Third Person	____________	____________

3. In the following sentences circle the correct pronoun.

   a. Have (you / your) washed (he / him) before?

   b. (We / Us) usually fill the washtub together.

   c. (I / Me) can't find the scrub brush.

   d. Rex always hides (it / its) somewhere.

4. Imagine that you are washing Rex with the other children, and then write a sentence about it using both a *subject pronoun* and an *object pronoun*.

   ____

   ____

Lessons to Learn

Pronoun Review

Review It

Reviewing is at the heart of learning. See if you can answer the following questions.

What are the eight parts of speech?

What are the principal elements?

What is a sentence?

What are the four kinds of sentences?

Can you give an example of a declarative sentence?

Can you give an example of an interrogative sentence?

Learn It

Your teacher will direct you to fill in the blanks in the following charts with the correct subject and object pronouns.

Example:

Teacher: "What should I write here?" pointing to the third-person plural object pronoun.
Student 1 says "*them*." While your teacher writes *them* in the correct place on the board, you should fill in that space in your book.

Subject Pronouns

	Singular	Plural
First Person	I	we
Second Person	you	you
Third Person	he, she, it	they

Object Pronouns

	Singular	Plural
First Person		
Second Person		
Third Person		

Analyze It

Analyze the following sentences (*S* = subject; *PV* = predicate verb; *hv* = helping verb; *adv* = adverb; *adj* = adjective; *do* = direct object).

1. Soon we should be returning him.

2. Will you recount them again?

Lessons to Practice

Pronoun Review

1. Analyze the following sentences (*S* = subject; *PV* = predicate verb; *hv* = helping verb; *adv* = adverb; *adj* = adjective; *do* = direct object).

   a. I did not ask them earlier.

   b. Quietly they whispered together.

   c. Did we want her along anyway?

   d. She should have stayed behind.

2. Fill in the following chart with the correct subject pronouns.

Subject Pronouns

	Singular	Plural
First Person	I	we
Second Person	you	you
Third Person	he, she, it	they

3. In the following sentences, circle the correct pronoun.

   a. Are (your / you) going tomorrow?

   b. (Her / She) left earlier today.

   c. (I / Me) will play soccer afterwards.

   d. Later the coach called (we / us) together.

4. Imagine that you're part of the soccer team and the coach called you over. Then, write a sentence using both a *subject pronoun* and an *object pronoun*.

I used his ball a dribbled over to the coach

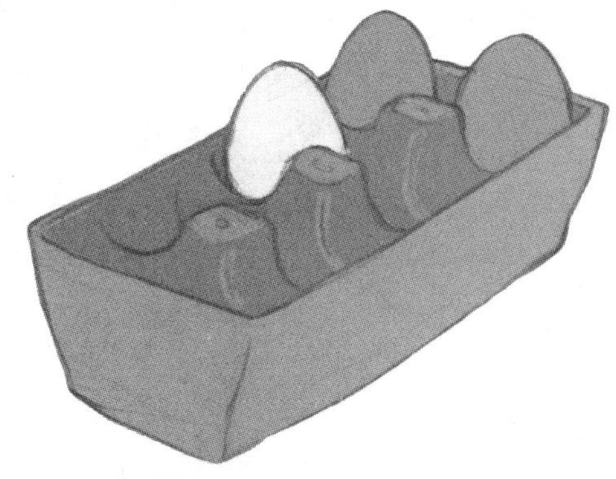

Lessons to Learn

Pronoun Review

Review It

Have you memorized the answers to the following questions yet? What is a pronoun? What are the subject pronouns? What are the object pronouns? What is an antecedent?

Learn It

1. The following chart organizes subject pronouns and object pronouns in a different way than you're used to seeing. This chart includes **gender**, which refers to whether the pronoun replaces a male, female, or **neuter** antecedent. Something that is neuter is neither male nor female. See if you can fill in the missing pronouns in the chart.

Number	Person	Gender	Subject Pronoun	Object Pronoun
Singular	first	male/female	I	me
	second	male/female	you	you
	third	male	he	his
	3	female	she	her
	3	neuter	it	it
Plural	first	male/female	we	us
	second	male/female	you	you
	third	male/female/ neuter	they	them

2. Imagine Heidi in art class holding a paintbrush and working on the clay pot she made. Then, write a sentence about it, being sure to include both a subject pronoun and an object pronoun.

Analyze It

Analyze the following sentences (*S* = subject; *PV* = predicate verb; *hv* = helping verb; *adv* = adverb; *adj* = adjective; *do* = direct object).

1. Must we always wear them?

2. I did not wear it yesterday.

Lessons to Practice

Pronoun Review

1. Analyze the following sentences (*S* = subject; *PV* = predicate verb; *hv* = helping verb; *adv* = adverb; *adj* = adjective; *do* = direct object).

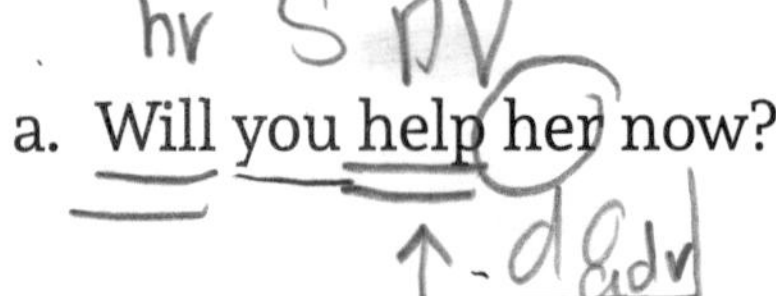

a. Will you help her now?

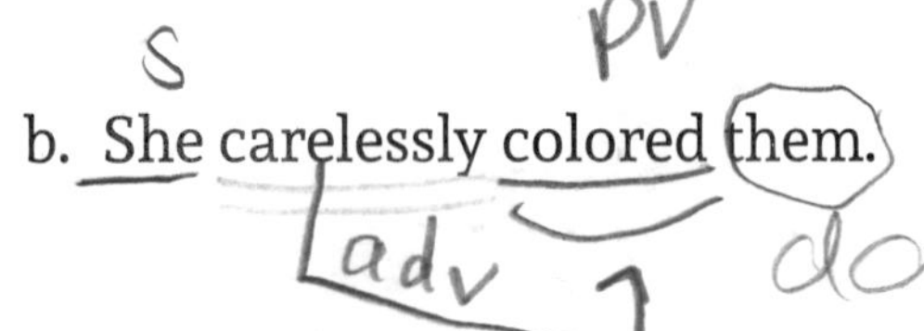

b. She carelessly colored them.

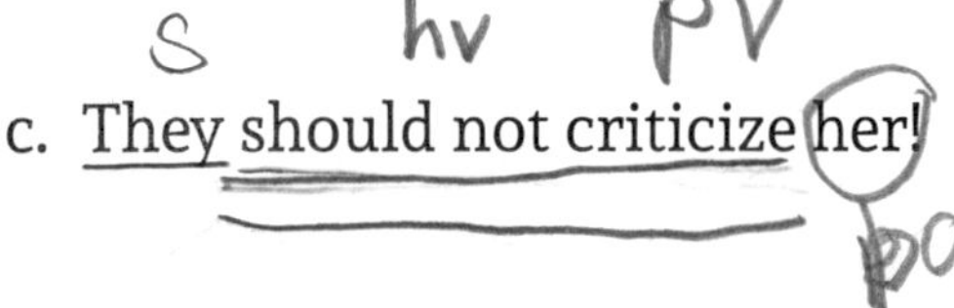

c. They should not criticize her!

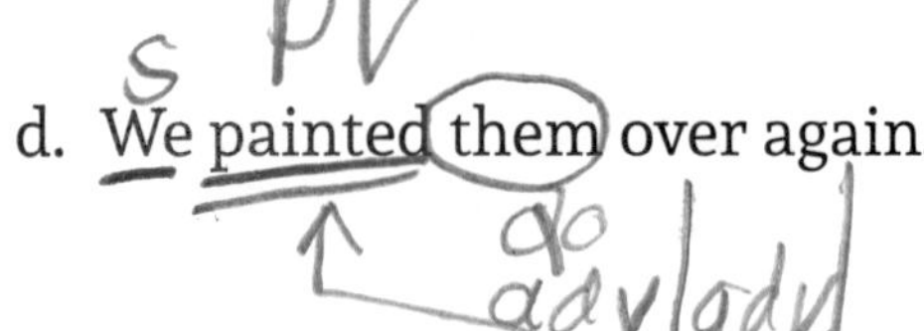

d. We painted them over again.

2. What is a pronoun?

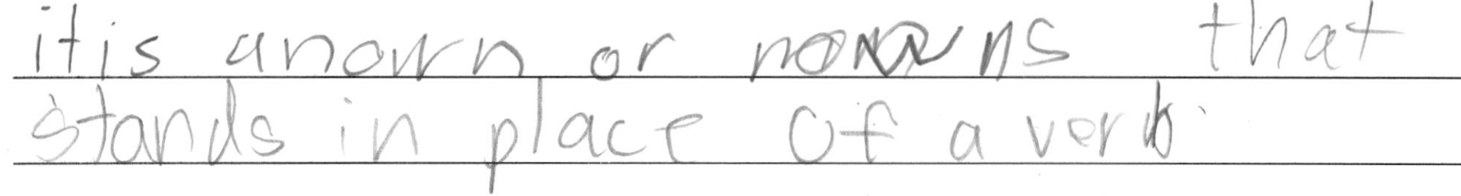

3. In the following sentences, circle the correct pronoun
   a. (I / He) shoots the basketball well.
   b. (They / Them) cheer loudly together.
   c. (You / He) usually sit alone.
   d. (We / She) carefully watches the game.
4. Imagine Winston shooting baskets with the basketball team, and then write an interrogative sentence about it using both a subject pronoun and an object pronoun.

Did he pass to him and
Did winston score

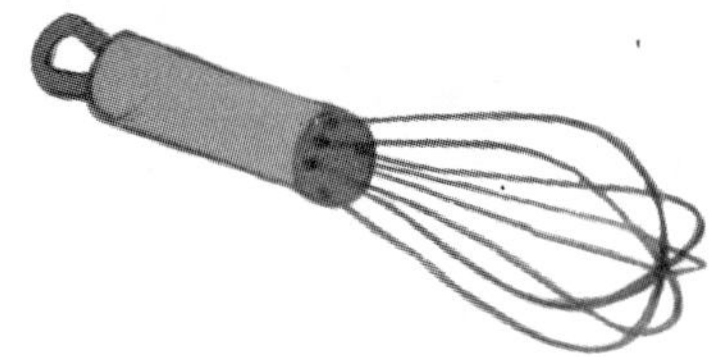

Review It

Answer the following review questions.

What are the eight parts of speech?

What is a sentence?

What is a declarative sentence?

What is an interrogative sentence?

What is an imperative sentence?

What is an exclamatory sentence?

What are the eight subject pronouns?

What are the eight object pronouns?

Learn It

Construct three sentences using the pronouns and transitive verbs listed in the following chart. Make sure that each sentence has a subject, verb, and direct object. You may also add more words, such as helping verbs or adverbs, to your sentences. Tell a mini story by making the topics of your sentences related. For an extra challenge, make one sentence declarative, one interrogative, and one exclamatory.

Example: *I* (subject pronoun), *remove* (verb), *it* (object pronoun).
Sentence: May *I remove it* now?

Subject Pronouns	Verbs	Object Pronouns
I	remove	me
you	shake	you
he	command	him
she	recount	her
it	fry	it
we	respect	us

Subject Pronouns	Verbs	Object Pronouns
you	draw	you
they	fill	them
I	answers	it
you	choose	her
we	write	you

1. He did not like the spooky turkey in my soup

2. Mom hates a fat frog in my shouses

3. My Dog doese not like a barking fog On the moon

Lessons to Practice—Review

Pronoun Review

1. Analyze the following sentences (*S* = subject; *PV* = predicate verb; *hv* = helping verb; *adv* = adverb; *adj* = adjective; *do* = direct object).

   a. He roughly put it down.

   b. We should have cared too.

   c. Could you put them safely away?

   d. Yesterday I accidentally broke them.

2. Fill in the following chart with the correct object pronouns.

Object Pronouns

	Singular	Plural
First Person		
Second Person		
Third Person		

3. In the following sentences, circle the correct pronoun.
   a. Did (us / we) read that same book last summer?
   b. Peggy whispers (he / it) softly.
   c. (Her / She) had a reason.
   d. Will (they / them) read (us / it) together again?
4. Imagine that you are with Peggy in class and you are reading the same book. Write a sentence about it using both a *subject pronoun* and an *object pronoun*.

   She read a page to me

Lessons to Enjoy—Poem
Pronoun Review

Some poems use silly words, and some poems use unusual ones. This poem, "Calico Pie," is a nonsense poem; it really doesn't make sense, but it's clever. Edward Lear, the British author, penned many such nonsensical poems that were whimsical (playful) and imaginative. Calico is a type of spotted cat or cotton cloth with a pattern printed on it. Do you think this poem is about a cat?

Calico Pie

by Edward Lear (1812–1888)

Calico Pie,
The little Birds fly
Down to the calico tree,
Their wings were blue,
And they sang, "Tilly-loo!"
Till away they flew—
And they never came back to me!
They never came back!
They never came back!
They never came back to me!

Calico Jam,
The little Fish swam
Over the syllabub sea,
He took off his hat,
To the Sole and the Sprat,
And the Willeby-wat—
But he never came back to me!
He never came back!
He never came back!
He never came back to me!

syllabub: a drink made with milk or cream mixed and sweetened with cider or wine

Calico Ban,
The little Mice ran,
To be ready in time for tea,
Flippity flup,
They drank it all up,
And danced in the cup—
But they never came back to me!
They never came back!
They never came back!
They never came back to me!

Calico Drum,
The Grasshoppers come,
The Butterfly, Beetle, and Bee,
Over the ground,
Around and around,
With a hop and a bound—
But they never came back to me!
They never came back!
They never came back![1]

bound: jump forward

Questions to Ponder

1. What kinds of animals never return?
2. What are "the Sole and the Sprat"?
3. What do you think a "Willeby-wat" is?
4. What are the pronouns in the poem?

1. Edward Lear, "Calico Pie," *The Golden Treasury of Poetry*, ed. Louis Untermeyer (New York: Golden Books Publishing, 1998), p. 211.

Chapter 3

Prepositional Phrases—Adverbial

Imagine plump apples hanging on tree branches in an orchard. If you could picture one tree from that orchard, thoughts of dozens of reddish-green apples clustering all over its leafy boughs might come to mind. Think about all that luscious (very delicious) fruit clinging to the branches. How is it attached to the tree? Each fleshy, round apple is connected to the tree by a slender stem. But if you subtract that stem, the apple falls to the ground with a thud. It is interesting to think that such a little twig could be so important, but without those itty-bitty stems, the tree would be fruitless.

Now imagine that a sentence is like that apple tree. You know a lot about the parts of this tree because you already have studied five of the eight parts of speech—nouns, verbs, adjectives, adverbs, and pronouns. In this chapter, you will learn about prepositions. A **preposition** connects a noun or pronoun to another word in the sentence, telling us something more about it. You can imagine the preposition as that important little stem that connects an apple (a noun or pronoun) to the branch (another word in the sentence).

Ideas to Understand

Before we define "preposition" further, take a peek at a list of some of the most common prepositions, and you will find them very familiar. You use them all the time to connect words within your sentences:

aboard	about	above	across	after
against	along	among	around	at
before	behind	below	beneath	beside
between	beyond	by	down	during
except	for	from	inside	in
into	near	of	off	on
out	outside	over	past	since
through	throughout	to	toward	under
up	until	upon	with	within
without	underneath			

To the Source:

■ **preposition**

In Latin, the word *preposition* is *praeponere*, which literally means "put before," with *prae* meaning "before" and *ponere* meaning "to put, set, or place."

A preposition■ is a word placed before a noun or pronoun (called the object of the preposition). Together they form a **prepositional phrase**. The preposition connects its object to another word in the sentence, often the verb. The preposition shows the relationship between the two words. That relationship might have to do with location: Mom put the apple pie (where?) *on the table*. It might have to do with time: We ate dessert (when?) *during the movie*. It might have to do with manner: We smacked our lips (how?) *with delight*. Whatever the relationship, the entire prepositional phrase modifies the word to which it is connected, such as the verb *put*, *ate*, or *smacked* in our sample sentences. In this way, the prepositional phrase behaves like a single part of speech. In *WOL Level 1*, we will be looking at prepositional phrases that behave like adverbs modifying verbs, and in *WOL Level 2*, we will include prepositional phrases behaving like adjectives.

Let's see how prepositional phrases function in an excerpt from the poem "Moon Folly" by Fannie Stearns Davis. (You can find the whole poem in The Curious Child's Literary Appendix.) The poet uses prepositional phrases that behave like adverbs, or **adverbial prepositional phrases**, to describe a night journey to capture the moon:

> I will go up the mountain after the Moon:
> She is caught in a dead fir-tree.
> Like a great pale apple of silver and pearl,
> Like a great pale apple is she.

I will leap and will clasp her with quick cold hands
And carry her home in my sack.
I will set her down safe on the oaken bench
That stands at the chimney-back.

And then I will sit by the fire all night,
And sit by the fire all day.
I will gnaw at the Moon to my heart's delight,
Till I gnaw her slowly away.[1]

Did you see any adverbial prepositional phrases in this portion of the poem? "With quick cold hands" describes *how* the poet will catch the moon, and "in my sack" describes *where* the poet carries the moon. If she had included "during the night," she would have told *when* the journey happened. These phrases are called adverbial prepositional phrases. Each one includes a preposition—*with*, *in*, or *during*—which we imagine to be like the connecting stem of an apple. Each preposition is followed by a noun, which is the object of the preposition—*hands*, *sack*, or *night*—which we have compared to the apple itself. Each phrase contains adjectives—*quick*, *cold*, *my*, *the*—which are a bit like the apple's leaves attached to an apple stem. What does the stem connect the apple to? In each of these examples, the stem connects the apple to a verb. That means each entire prepositional phrase functions as an adverb modifying the verb.

Keep in mind that the noun or pronoun in a prepositional phrase is called the object of the preposition. Most objects of the preposition are common nouns. **Common nouns** name any person, place, thing, or idea. *Apple* and *hands* are common nouns because they name a nonspecific person or thing. Some objects of the prepositions are proper nouns. **Proper nouns**, such as the months of the year, refer to a particular person, place, thing, or idea; they begin with a capital letter.

Your goal for this lesson is to learn to identify prepositions, their objects, and what they modify in sentences. The prepositions listed on the previous page are the most common ones used in English. Being able to recognize them at a glance is a handy analytic skill, so you will need to memorize them.

1. Fannie Stearns Davis, "Moon Folly" from *In Poetry*, vol. I, ed. Harriet Monroe (New York: A.M.S. Reprint CO, Vol. 1, No. 6, March 1912–1913), pp. 183–184. Available at: https://books.google.com/books?id=9MARAAAAYAAJ.

Terms to Remember

By now you know that music is one of the best tools for memorizing. The long list of prepositions and the related definitions will be a snap once you learn the tunes.

NEW! **Preposition** *(1–16)*

A preposition *(a preposition)*
is a part of speech *(is a part of speech)*
used to show the relationship
between certain words in a sentence *(in a sentence). (Repeat.)*

NEW! **List of Prepositions** *(1–17)*

Aboard, about, above, across, after, against, along, among, around
Preposition Words
Before, behind, below, beneath, beside, between, beyond, at, by
Preposition Words
Down, during, except, for, from, inside, in, into, near
Preposition Words
Of, off, on, out, outside, over, past, since, through
Preposition Words
Throughout, to, toward,
Under, up, until,
Upon, with, within,
Without, underneath
Preposition Words
Preposition Words
Preposition Words!

NEW! **Phrase** *(1–18)*

A phrase is a group of words
behaving like one part of speech
not containing a subject or a predicate. *(Repeat.)*

NEW! Object of the Preposition *(1–19)*

The object of the preposition
The object of the preposition
is the noun or pronoun
after the preposition. *(Repeat.)*

A Sentence to Analyze

In this chapter, we are adding another level of analysis that comes *before* the steps that you are used to doing. When you are analyzing sentences that contain prepositional phrases, you need to first mark the parts of a prepositional phrase—the preposition, the object of the preposition, any adjectives within the phrase—so that you can analyze the whole phrase as a modifier within the sentence.

So, from now on your analysis of sentences will follow what we call the **order of analysis**. The order is phrases, clauses, principal elements, and modifiers. As you say the analysis aloud and mark the sentence, the order of analysis falls into two parts:

Part 1: Identify the *phrases*. (You will learn how to identify *clauses* later in *WOL Level 2*.)

Part 2: Identify the *principal elements* and *modifiers*.

After you read aloud the sentence to analyze, recite the following chant to help you remember this organizing principle: "The order of analysis is phrases, clauses, principal elements, modifiers."

Part 1: Identify Phrases

Winston paddled(to the island)
p adj op

a. (First, read the sentence aloud.) "Winston paddled to the island."

b. Chant: "The order of analysis is phrases, clauses, principal elements, modifiers."

c. "Are there any prepositional phrases?" (Choral response: "Yes, sir." Since there is one in this sentence, you can answer *yes*.)

d. "*To the island* is a prepositional phrase." (Since *to the island* is a prepositional phrase, put parentheses around the phrase.)

e. "*To* is the preposition." (Since *to* is a preposition, you can place a lowercase letter *p* underneath it.)
"*Island* is the object of the preposition." (Since *island* is a noun and is connected to the preposition, making it the object of the preposition, you can place the lowercase letters *op* underneath it.)

f. "*The* is an adjective."[2] (Since *the* tells *which* island, it is an adjective. You can draw a straight line down from the adjective, then a horizontal line toward the word it modifies, and then a straight line with an arrow pointing to *island*. Write *adj* in lowercase letters in the elbow opposite the line with the arrow.)

Part 2: Identify Principal Elements and Modifiers

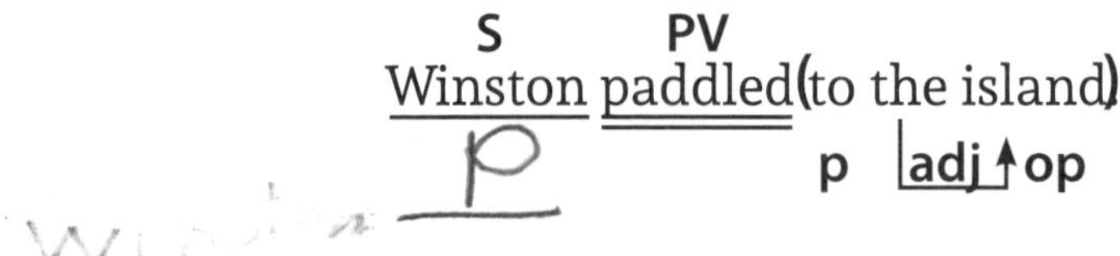

a. (Read the sentence again aloud.) "Winston paddled to the island."

b. "This is a sentence and it is declarative."

c. "This sentence is about *Winston*. So, Winston is the subject because it is what the sentence is about." (Since *Winston* is the subject, underline the word and place a capital letter *S* above it.)

d. "This sentence tells us that Winston *paddled*. So, *paddled* is the predicate because it is what the sentence tells us about *Winston*." (Since *paddled* tells us something about Winston, double underline the predicate and place a capital letter *P* above it.)

e. "It is a predicate verb because it shows action. There is no linking verb because predicate verbs do not need linking verbs." (Since *paddled* shows action, place a capital letter *V* to the right of the letter *P* above the predicate.)

2. The words *article adjective* can be substituted in place of the word *adjective*.

f. "*To the island* tells us *where* Winston paddled." (Since *to the island* tells *where* Winston paddled, you can draw a straight line down from the letter *p* that's under the preposition, then a horizontal line toward the word that it modifies, and then a straight line with an arrow pointing to *paddled.*)

g. "So, *to the island* is an adverbial element because it modifies a verb. It is an adverbial prepositional phrase." (Since the prepositional phrase is behaving like an adverb, write *adv* in lowercase letters in the elbow opposite the line with the arrow. Since the phrase is a prepositional phrase, you can write *prep* in lowercase letters directly below the *adv*, underneath the modifier line.)

If you first identify and analyze in a sentence the prepositional phrases with their slender stems (the preposition) and their apples (the noun/pronoun as object of the preposition), you can identify the principal elements of the sentence more promptly.

Turn back to the illustration of the three siblings under an apple tree. Did you notice the wooden bench? Do you think the children are picking apples in the park or are they somewhere else? Where are apples usually grown? Have you ever picked apples?

Review It

Can you name the forty-seven prepositions you have learned in this chapter? Learn the song and you will be able to say all of them by heart.

aboard	about	above	across	after
against	along	among	around	at
before	behind	below	beneath	beside
between	beyond	by	down	during
except	for	from	inside	in
into	near	of	off	on
out	outside	over	past	since
through	throughout	to	toward	under
up	until	upon	with	within
without	underneath			

Learn It

Knowing the prepositions will make it easier for you to find prepositional phrases in sentences. In the following sentences, find the prepositions and then put parentheses around the prepositional phrases.

Example: The dark gray clouds filled the sky (in the west).

1. The green banners decorated the gate with school colors.
2. Peggy is now playing soccer with Heidi after school.
3. The coach might run with the team tonight.
4. Unfortunately an unforeseen storm drove them into the shelter.

Introductory Lesson
Prepositional Phrases—Adverbial

Analyze It

Analyze the following sentences (*S* = subject; *PV* = predicate verb; *hv* = helping verb; *adv* = adverb; *adj* = adjective; *do* = direct object; *p* = preposition; *op* = object of the preposition; *prep* = prepositional phrase).

1. We ate popcorn during the movie.

2. Some people crunched potato chips throughout it.

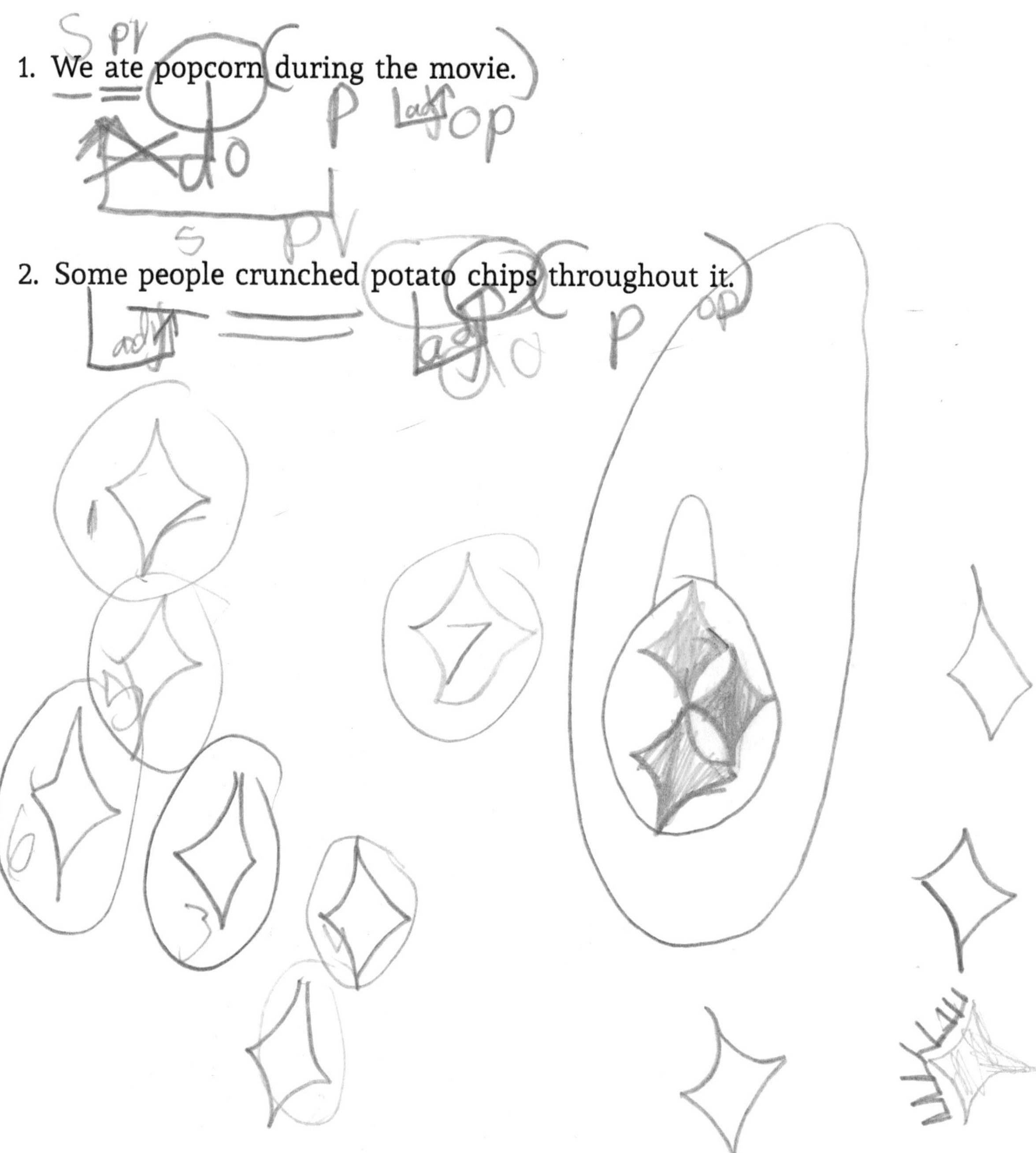

Introductory Practice
Prepositional Phrases—Adverbial

1. Analyze the following sentences (*S* = subject; *PV* = predicate verb; *hv* = helping verb; *adv* = adverb; *adj* = adjective; *do* = direct object; *p* = preposition; *op* = object of the preposition; *prep* = prepositional phrase).

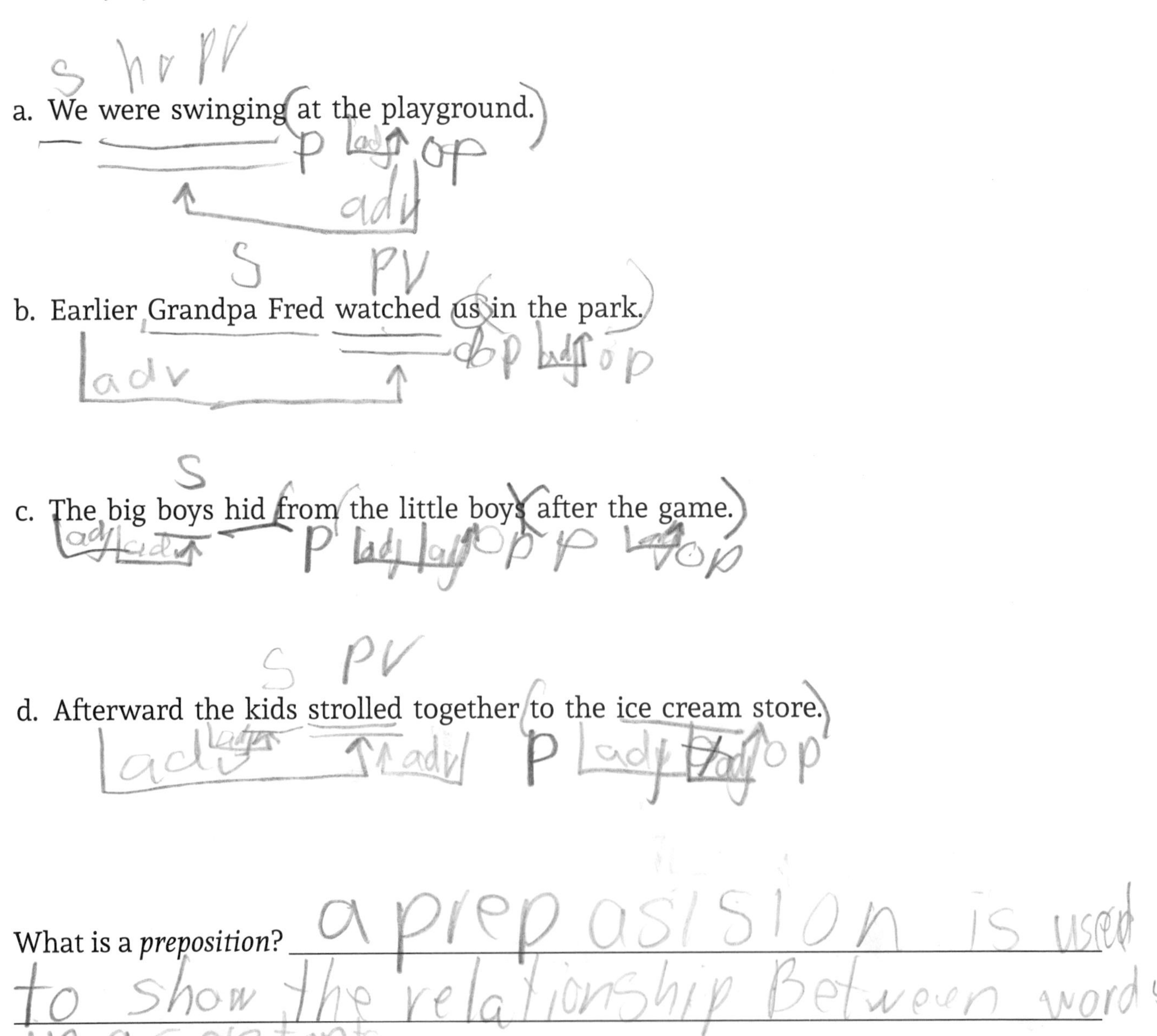

a. We were swinging at the playground.

b. Earlier Grandpa Fred watched us in the park.

c. The big boys hid from the little boys after the game.

d. Afterward the kids strolled together to the ice cream store.

2. What is a *preposition*? ____

3. List nine prepositions that begin with the letter *a*.

My name is Bobby

Notes

Lessons to Learn
Prepositional Phrases—Adverbial

Review It

Prepositions are little words, but they are very important in our English language. What is a preposition? Can you name all the prepositions that begin with the letter *a*? What about listing the ones beginning with the letter *b*? What is a phrase? What is an object of the preposition?

Learn It

Each sentence below is missing two things that every sentence should have: a capital letter at the beginning and a period at the end. Since they contain at least one month of the year, these particular sentences are also missing something in the middle: a capital letter at the beginning of that proper noun. On the lines provided, correct all of the following sentences by rewriting them with the proper capitalization and punctuation.

Example: school begins in september
School begins in September .

1. the month of september has thirty days

The month of September
has thirdy days

2. april also has the same number of days as september

April also has the same
number of days as September

3. remember the number of days in april is the same as in june

4. is the number of days in november the same as in june too

Analyze It

Analyze the following sentences (*S* = subject; *PV* = predicate verb; *hv* = helping verb; *adv* = adverb; *adj* = adjective; *do* = direct object; *p* = preposition; *op* = object of the preposition; *prep* = prepositional phrase).

1. The shepherd led the sheep to the pasture.

2. Foolishly the boy planned a mean trick during the afternoon.

Lessons to Practice
Prepositional Phrases—Adverbial

1. Analyze the following sentences (*S* = subject; *PV* = predicate verb; *hv* = helping verb; *adv* = adverb; *adj* = adjective; *do* = direct object; *p* = preposition; *op* = object of the preposition; *prep* = prepositional phrase).

   a. Lucy will not leave for school without the note.

   b. Earlier she forgot the envelope on the counter.

   c. Mom reminded her again about the note.

   d. Cleverly she placed it in the lunchbox.

2. On the lines provided, correct all of the following sentences by rewriting them with the proper capitalization and punctuation. Remember that the months of the year are proper nouns.

   a. gentle april showers often bring may flowers

b. do goldenrods and sword lilies dot the august gardens

Do Goldenrods and sword lilies dot the august gardens?

c. yellow mums are also called painted daisies in september

yellow mums are also caled painted daisies in september

d. february displays her ice crystals and snow dainties

February displays her ice crystals and snow dainties

3. Imagine that at lunchtime Lucy finds the note she was looking for. Now write a sentence about it, being sure to include a prepositional phrase.

She found it in her lunch. Box

Lessons to Learn

Prepositional Phrases—Adverbial

Review It

Practice makes perfect. Can you answer the following questions?

What is a preposition?

What is an object of the preposition?

What is a phrase?

What are the forty-seven prepositions you've learned in this chapter?

Learn It

On the lines provided, correct all of the following sentences by rewriting them with the proper capitalization and punctuation. Remember that the months of the year are proper nouns.

Example: spring begins in march **Spring begins in March.**

1. january has thirty-one days

   Januaryhas thirty-one days.

2. december and july both have as many days as january

   December and July Both have as many days as January

3. march and may have as many days as august and july

   March and May have as many days as Augest and July

4. curiously february only has twenty-eight days

5. february has twenty-nine days every four years

Analyze It

Analyze the following sentences (*S* = subject; *PV* = predicate verb; *hv* = helping verb; *adv* = adverb; *adj* = adjective; *do* = direct object; *p* = preposition; *op* = object of the preposition; *prep* = prepositional phrase).

1. Did Davy Crockett fight a bear in the woods?

2. Is Dad reading adventure tales to the children again?

Lessons to Practice B

Prepositional Phrases—Adverbial

1. Analyze the following sentences (*S* = subject; *PV* = predicate verb; *hv* = helping verb; *adv* = adverb; *adj* = adjective; *do* = direct object; *p* = preposition; *op* = object of the preposition; *prep* = prepositional phrase).

   a. The farmer carefully drove the old tractor from the barn to the field.

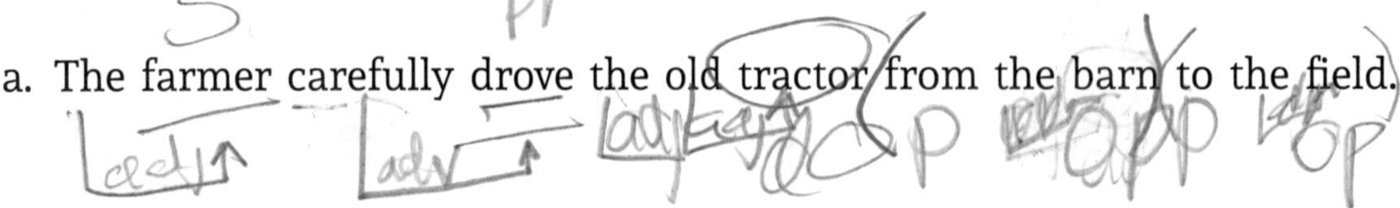

   b. Quickly four mice scurried through the grass to the farm shed.

   c. Two mice families live underneath the front porch.

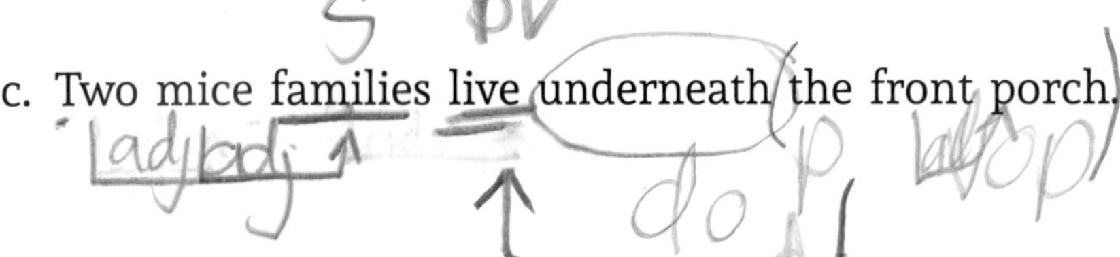

   d. Those tiny, furry creatures ate all the seeds under the birdfeeder.

2. On the lines provided, correct all of the following sentences by rewriting them with the proper capitalization and punctuation. Remember that the months of the year are proper nouns.

   a. are the trees and flowers really sleeping in january

   Are the trees and flowers really sleeping in January?

b. november winds blow oak leaves and ash leaves about

November winds blow oak leaves and ash leaves about!

c. tulips and crocuses grow in march

Tulips and Crocuses grow in March.

d. lily pads and water lilies float on the quiet pond in july

Lily pads and watter lilies float on the quiet pont in July

3. List nine prepositions that *do not* begin with the letter *a*.

Befor	Beneath	Below
By	Beond	Beside
Between	Behind	up

Lessons to Learn
Prepositional Phrases—Adverbial

Review It

Reviewing is the backbone of learning new terms, so let's review some of the things you've learned:

Define a preposition.

List all of the prepositions that begin with the letter *t*.

What is a phrase?

What is the definition of object of the preposition?

Learn It

1. Prepositions are connector words. They join the noun or pronoun that is the object of the preposition with another word in the sentence. Fill in the missing preposition in each of the following sentences to show the relationship between the object of the preposition and the verb.

Example: The raindrops dripped ___down___ the windowpane.

a. Several sailboats are anchored ___in___ the bay.

b. Peggy walked ___with___ an umbrella during the April showers.

c. Many children watched the rain ___from___ the shelter.

d. Suddenly Rex escaped ___Behind___ the house.

e. Heidi called ___the___ the naughty dog.

f. She slipped ___in___ a puddle.

Lessons to Learn

Prepositional Phrases—Adverbial

g. Fortunately Theo grabbed Rex ____________ the collar.

h. Theo dried Rex ____________ an old beach towel.

2. Write a sentence about Rex and the rainy day, being sure to include a prepositional phrase in your sentence.

____

____

Analyze It

Analyze the following sentences (*S* = subject; *PV* = predicate verb; *hv* = helping verb; *adv* = adverb; *adj* = adjective; *do* = direct object; *p* = preposition; *op* = object of the preposition; *prep* = prepositional phrase).

1. The curious toddler tripped over it in the kitchen.

2. Unfortunately he spilled the water on the floor.

Lessons to Practice

Prepositional Phrases—Adverbial

1. Analyze the following sentences (*S* = subject; *PV* = predicate verb; *hv* = helping verb; *adv* = adverb; *adj* = adjective; *do* = direct object; *p* = preposition; *op* = object of the preposition; *prep* = prepositional phrase).

   a. Yesterday Grandma Lola bought peaches from the market.

   b. She is baking peach pies in the kitchen for the boys.

   c. Later Mom will sell the pies at the bake sale for the team.

   d. The basketball team is raising money for new jerseys.

2. What is a *preposition*? it is used to show the relation ship between certain words in a sentence

3. Imagine the whole team is at the next game and they are all wearing their new jerseys. Write a sentence about it, being sure to use a prepositional phrase in it.

   look at the Jersey namber witch is clean

Notes

Review It

Answer the following review questions:

What is a preposition?

What is a phrase?

What is an object of the preposition?

Can you name the forty-seven prepositions you have learned in this chapter?

Learn It

Play the review game Lightning by using some of the following prepositions in sentences. Your teacher will say a preposition, and a student has five seconds to think of an object of the preposition.

Example:

Teacher: "to"
Student: "*to the shore*"

aboard	about	above	across	after
against	along	among	around	at
before	behind	below	beneath	beside
between	beyond	by	down	during
except	for	from	inside	in
into	near	of	off	on
out	outside	over	past	since
through	throughout	to	toward	under
up	until	upon	with	within
without	underneath			

Write a sentence using one of the prepositional phrases from the Lightning game.

____

____

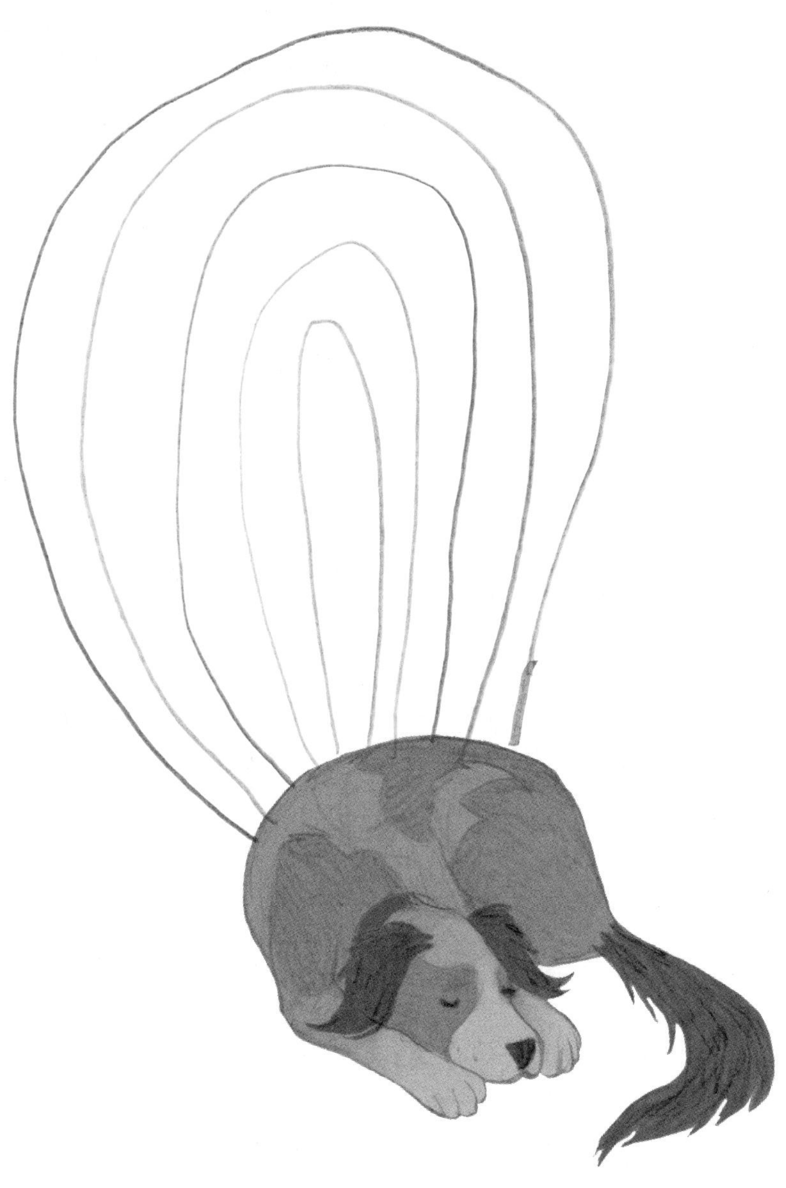

Lessons to Practice—Review

Prepositional Phrases—Adverbial

1. Analyze the following sentences: (*S* = subject; *PV* = predicate verb; *hv* = helping verb; *adv* = adverb; *adj* = adjective; *do* = direct object; *p* = preposition; *op* = object of the preposition; *prep* = prepositional phrase).

   a. Icicles slowly dripped from the rooftop outside.

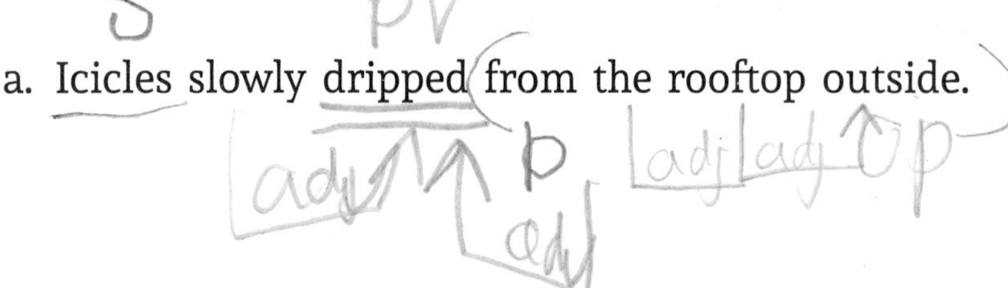

   b. The tiny snowflakes are dancing around the pine tree too.

   c. Did Jack Frost paint on the window those icy designs?

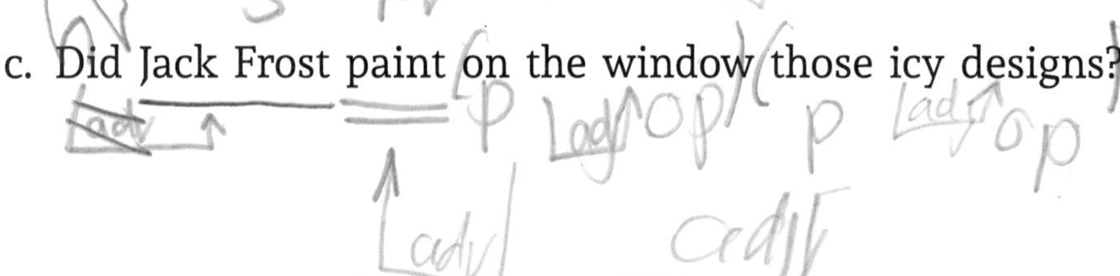

   d. Now the winter winds are blowing the snow into giant drifts.

2. On the lines provided, correct all of the following sentences by rewriting them with the proper capitalization and punctuation. Remember that the months of the year are proper nouns.

   a. red and white roses creep along the wooden fences in june

   Red and white roses creep along the wooden fences in June.

b. orange pumpkins grow rounder during colorful october

Orange pumpkins grow rounder durring colerful October.

c. will may be robed in her flowered dress once more

Will May be robed in her flowered dress once more?

d. holly and ivy are twisted into wreaths in december

holly and ivy are twisted into wreaths in December.

3. List nine prepositions.

befor	Behind	Below
beneath	becided	Between
beyound	at	by

Lessons to Enjoy—Poem
Prepositional Phrases—Adverbial

What do you think of when you imagine a snowy winter day? Do you think of crunching snow? Or do you think of using the frosty air to blow clouds of smoke like a dragon? Elinor Wylie writes of a walk with a friend on a snowy day. What kinds of shoes do they imagine they wear to walk in the snow?

Velvet Shoes

by Elinor Wylie (1885–1928)

tranquil: peaceful
pace: speed at which something moves
shod: wearing shoes

Let us walk in the white snow
In a soundless space;
With footsteps quiet and slow;
At a tranquil pace,
Under veils of white lace.

I shall go shod in silk,
And you in wool,
White as a white cow's milk,
More beautiful
Than the breast of a gull.

down: soft feathers from the underside of a goose or duck
fleece: the soft wool of a sheep
velvet: a soft, thick, expensive fabric

We shall walk through the still town
In a windless peace;
We shall step upon white down
Upon silver fleece,
Upon softer than these.

We shall walk in velvet shoes;
Wherever we go
Silence will fall like dews
On white silence below,
We shall walk in the snow.[1]

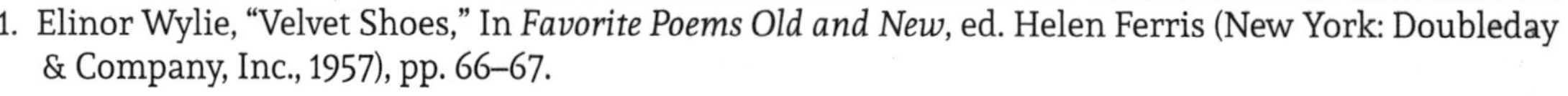

1. Elinor Wylie, "Velvet Shoes," In *Favorite Poems Old and New*, ed. Helen Ferris (New York: Doubleday & Company, Inc., 1957), pp. 66–67.

Questions to Ponder

1. What does "I shall go shod in silk and you in wool" mean?
2. To what white things is the snow compared?
3. Which words in the poem describe the silence of the snowy scene?
4. To whom do you think the speaker is speaking in the poem?

Chapter 4

Introductory Prepositional Phrases

In the morning when you put on your shoes, do you put on one sock and one shoe and then put on the second sock and second shoe? Or do you put both socks on first before putting on your shoes? While it's obviously important that you not put a sock on over a shoe, the order in which you put on your socks and then your shoes isn't really all that important. It's up to you what order you do it in. Prepositional phrases are kind of like socks and shoes: When they behave like adverbs, as they often do, they can be put in a different order in a sentence. For instance, an author might put the prepositional phrase at the beginning of the sentence or at the end or even in the middle. *In this chapter*, we will continue our study of adverbial prepositional phrases. We might even say that we will continue *in this chapter* our study of adverbial prepositional phrases. We could also say that we will continue our study of adverbial prepositional phrases *in this chapter*. Do you get the idea?

Ideas to Understand

An adverbial prepositional phrase behaves like an adverb even though the phrase is made up of several words. Most of the sentences we studied in the previous chapter included such phrases placed *after* the verb, a common position for the phrase because it functions as an adverb telling *where*, *when*, or *how* the verb does its action. In this chapter, you will learn that sometimes, for emphasis, a writer places a prepositional phrase at the beginning of the sentence. When it is in that position it is called an **introductory prepositional phrase** because it introduces the subject and the verb. A comma is often used after the introductory prep-

The animals' adventures in *The Wind in the Willows* started out as bedtime stories that Kenneth Grahame told his young son. After Grahame put them together as a novel in 1908, one of its biggest fans was Theodore Roosevelt, who was the president of the United States at the time. A children's novel that a president can love—give it a try! You may fall in love with Mole, Rat, Toad, and Badger too.

ositional phrase to separate it from the principal elements. That way it receives more attention than it would if placed after the verb.

In the following excerpt from his book *The Wind in the Willows*, Kenneth Grahame uses two introductory adverbial prepositional phrases, "In the winter time" and "During the short day," to describe Rat's day in winter.

> In the winter time the Rat slept a great deal, retiring early and rising late. During his short day he sometimes scribbled poetry or did other small domestic jobs about the house; and, of course, there were always animals dropping in for a chat, and consequently there was a good deal of storytelling and comparing notes on the past summer and all its doings.[1]

By using prepositional phrases at the beginning of two of his sentences, Grahame emphasizes that these particular activities happened on Rat's winter days and not during the summer. When an adverbial prepositional phrase is placed at the beginning of a sentence, more attention is drawn to it than when it is placed after the verb. If an author wants to emphasize the *how*, *when*, or *where* of a verb, she may choose to use an introductory prepositional phrase. Whether placed at the start of the sentence or after the verb, neither position is more correct than the other for an adverbial prepositional phrase; the writer gets to choose.

Terms to Remember

Do you have the most common prepositions all memorized yet? When you have mastered the preposition list, identifying a prepositional phrase in a sentence will be as easy as . . . well, as putting on your socks and shoes!

Preposition *(1–16)*

A preposition *(a preposition)*
is a part of speech *(is a part of speech)*
used to show the relationship
between certain words in a sentence *(in a sentence). (Repeat.)*

1. Kenneth Grahame "The Wild Wood," *The Wind in the Willows* (New York: The New American Library, Inc., 1969), pp. 56–57.

List of Prepositions *(1–17)*

Aboard, about, above, across, after, against, along, among, around
Preposition Words
Before, behind, below, beneath, beside, between, beyond, at, by
Preposition Words
Down, during, except, for, from, inside, in, into, near
Preposition Words
Of, off, on, out, outside, over, past, since, through
Preposition Words
Throughout, to, toward,
Under, up, until,
Upon, with, within,
Without, underneath
Preposition Words
Preposition Words
Preposition Words!

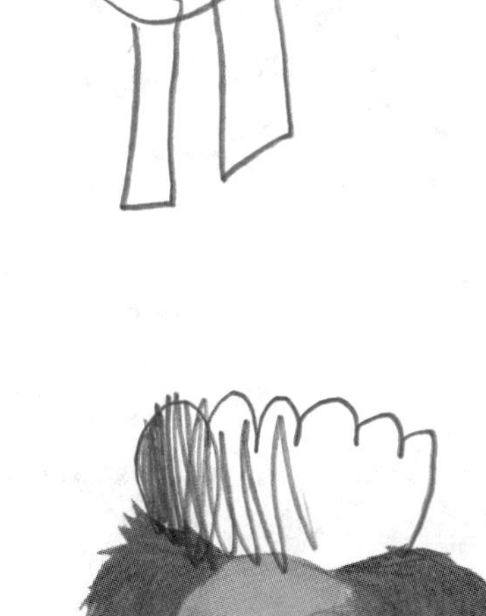

Object of the Preposition *(1–19)*

The object of the preposition
The object of the preposition
is the noun or pronoun
after the preposition. *(Repeat.)*

Sentences to Analyze

Make sure that you review the order of analysis chant: "The order of analysis is phrases, clauses, principal elements, modifiers." Remember that when you analyze sentences you need to complete the steps in the following order:

Part 1: Identify Phrases (Clauses will be included later.)

Part 2: Identify Principal Elements and Modifiers

Keep in mind that wherever prepositional phrases are located in a sentence, parentheses should be placed around them before you analyze the sentence. That way it is easier to identify

what the sentence is about (subject) and what the subject is doing (predicate verb). As you learned in chapter 3, all the markings are first written beneath the phrase; then, you go on to analyze the principal elements of the sentence and the modifiers. As you neatly mark the sentence, say the analysis aloud.

Part 1: Identify Phrases

(In the morning) Winston paddled along.
p adj op

a. (First, read the sentence aloud.) "In the morning, Winston paddled along."

b. "The order of analysis is phrases, clauses, principal elements, modifiers."

c. "Are there any prepositional phrases?" (Since there is one in this sentence, you can answer yes.)

d. "*In the morning* is a prepositional phrase." (Since *in the morning* is a prepositional phrase, put parentheses around it.)

e. "*In* is the preposition." (Since *in* is a preposition, you can place a lowercase letter *p* underneath it.)

f. "*Morning* is the object of the preposition." (Since *morning* is connected to the preposition and is therefore the object of the preposition, you can place the lowercase letters *op* underneath it.)

g. "*The* is an adjective."[2] (Since *the* tells which morning, it is an adjective. You can draw a straight line down from the adjective, then a horizontal line toward the word it modifies, and then a straight line with an arrow pointing to *morning*. Write *adj* in lowercase letters in the elbow opposite the line with the arrow.)

2. The words *article adjective* can be substituted in place of the word *adjective*.

Part 2: Identify Principal Elements and Modifiers

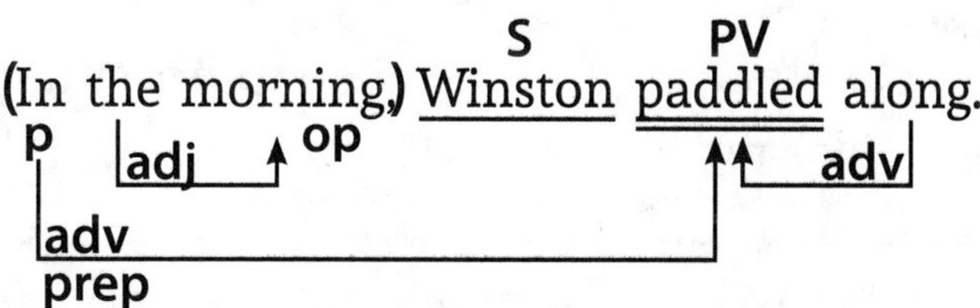

a. (Read the sentence again aloud.) "In the morning, Winston paddled along."

b. "This is a sentence and it is declarative."

c. "This sentence is about *Winston*. So, Winston is the subject because it is what the sentence is about." (Since *Winston* is the subject, underline the word and place a capital letter *S* above it.)

d. "This sentence tells us that Winston *paddled*. So, *paddled* is the predicate because it is what the sentence tells us about *Winston*." (Since *paddled* tells us something about Winston, double underline the predicate and place a capital letter *P* above it.)

e. "It is a predicate verb because it shows action. There is no linking verb because predicate verbs do not need linking verbs." (Since *paddled* shows action, place a capital letter *V* to the right of the letter *P* above the predicate.)

f. "*Along* tells us *where* Winston paddled. So, *along* is an adverbial element that modifies a verb. It is an adverb." (Since *along* is modifying where Winston is paddling, draw a straight line down from the adverb, then a horizontal line toward the word that it modifies, and then a straight line with an arrow pointing to the word it modifies. Place a lowercase *adv* in the elbow opposite the line with the arrow.)

g. "*In the morning* tells us *when* Winston paddled." (Since *in the morning* tells when Winston paddled, you can draw a straight line down from the letter *p* that's under the preposition, then a horizontal line toward the word that it modifies, and then a straight line with an arrow pointing to *paddled*.)

h. "So, *in the morning* is an adverbial element because it modifies a verb. It is an adverbial prepositional phrase." (Since the prepositional phrase is behaving like an adverb, write *adv* in lowercase letters in the elbow opposite the line with the arrow. Since the phrase is a prepositional phrase, you can write *prep* in lowercase letters directly below the *adv*, underneath the modifier line.)

In the previous chapter, you thought about prepositional phrases as apples and stems: The preposition is the little stem, and the noun or object of the preposition is the fruit. Now you see that the little stem can be attached to the branch in different places. When you are writing, you can choose where to put a prepositional phrase in your sentence for the best effect. *For greater emphasis*, the prepositional phrase comes at the beginning of the sentence. You can also put the prepositional phrase somewhere after the verb *in the more common position.* (Oh, look at those two sentences! What do you see?)

Notes

Introductory Lesson
Introductory Prepositional Phrases

Review It

Did you know that in the English language there are more than 100 prepositions? Most of them are not used very often, so for now you have to memorize only the most common ones. Recite all forty-seven of them.

Learn It

You learned in *WOL1A* that a sentence is a group of words expressing a complete thought. You also know that to be complete, the sentence needs both a subject and a predicate, the principal elements. A group of words that looks like a sentence, starting with a capital letter and ending with a period, is not a sentence if it is missing either a subject or a predicate—or both. Then it is called a **fragment**. You should avoid fragments in your writing.

Determine if the following groups of words are sentences or fragments and on the lines provided write *sentence* or *fragment* as appropriate.

Example: _____fragment_____ "Around the grayish-blue, rusty bike carrier." (This is a fragment since it does not have a subject and predicate.)

1. ____________________ On the old, yellow bicycle.
2. ____________________ Near the tall tower, the birds nested.
3. ____________________ Later after the girls' bike ride.
4. ____________________ Outside she cried.
5. ____________________ Throughout the ten miles of trails.
6. ____________________Suddenly Lucy hiccuped.

Analyze It

Analyze the following sentences (*S* = subject; *PV* = predicate verb; *hv* = helping verb; *adv* = adverb; *adj* = adjective; *do* = direct object; *p* = preposition; *op* = object of the preposition; *prep* = prepositional phrase).

1. At the soccer game, Winston ordered a hamburger.

2. By the afternoon, he asked for another sandwich.

Introductory Practice

Introductory Prepositional Phrases

1. Analyze the following sentences (*S* = subject; *PV* = predicate verb; *hv* = helping verb; *adv* = adverb; *adj* = adjective; *do* = direct object; *p* = preposition; *op* = object of the preposition; *prep* = prepositional phrase).

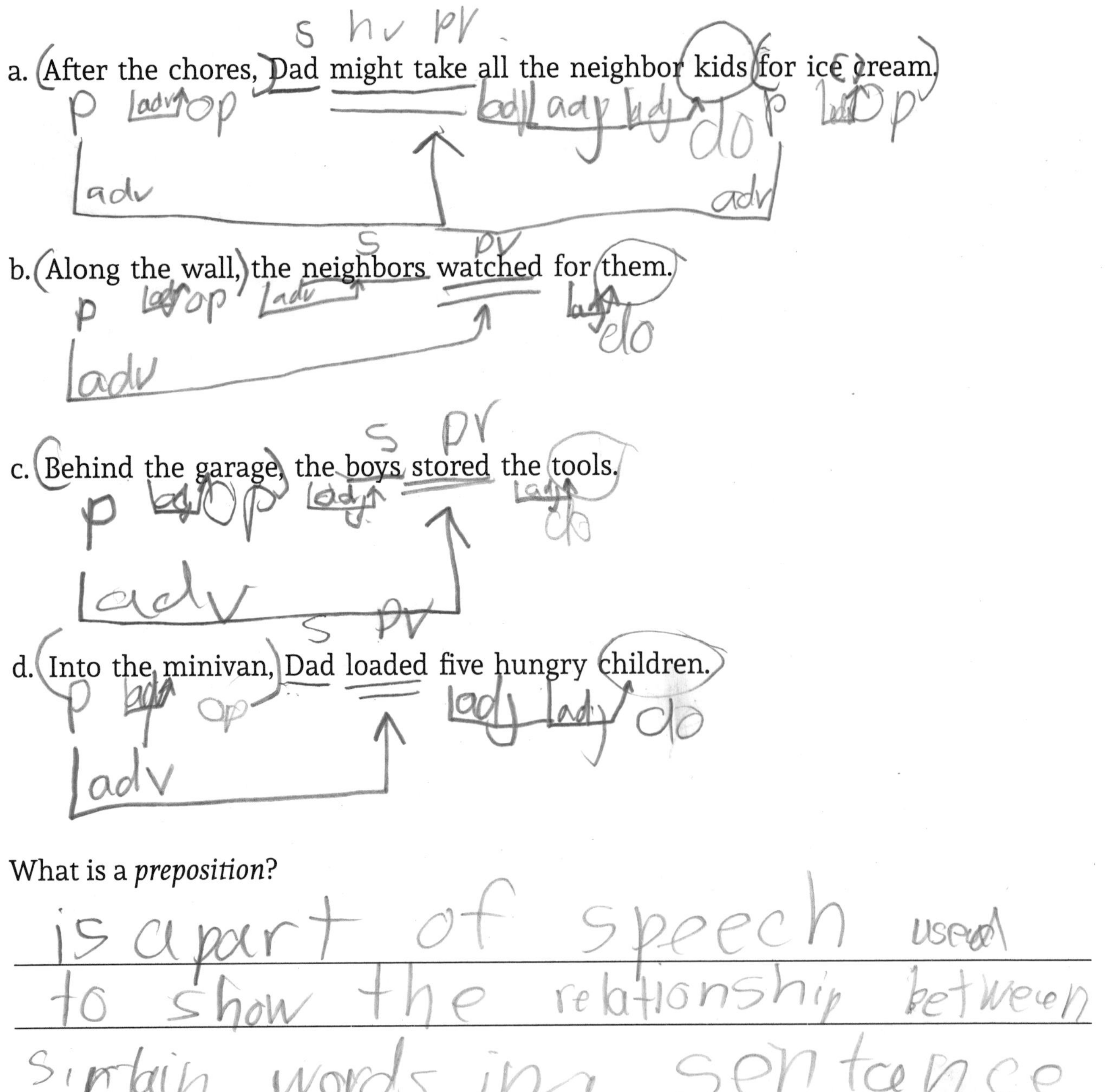

a. After the chores, Dad might take all the neighbor kids for ice cream.

b. Along the wall, the neighbors watched for them.

c. Behind the garage, the boys stored the tools.

d. Into the minivan, Dad loaded five hungry children.

2. What is a *preposition*?

3. Imagine that you are going for ice cream with your friends after doing chores. With that in mind, complete the phrase for each preposition listed, and then write a sentence that includes an introductory prepositional phrase.

Example: over ______________________
Sentence: *Over the railroad tracks,* **the van wheels rumbled.**

a. at the white board

Sentence: (At the white) board) I wrote a sum.

b. between to walls

Sentence: (between walls) that are clossing in

Review It

Prepositions are little words, but they are very important words in our English language. Without them, sentences would fall apart.

What is a preposition? Name twenty prepositions.

What is an object of the preposition?

Give an example of a sentence with a prepositional phrase placed after the verb.

Give an example of a sentence with an introductory prepositional phrase.

Learn It

Remember that a sentence is a group of words expressing a complete thought. It is a complete sentence only if it contains both a subject and a verb. Make the following fragments into complete sentences. As the writer, you get to choose whether the sentences have introductory prepositional phrases or not.

Example: "During lunch."
***During lunch,* the cousins planned the afternoon.**

1. underneath the clothes pile in the laundry room

____

____

2. throughout the long afternoon

____

____

3. in the sunlight near the window

____

____

4. between two huge sock piles

____

____

Analyze It

Analyze the following sentences (*S* = subject; *PV* = predicate verb; *hv* = helping verb; *adv* = adverb; *adj* = adjective; *do* = direct object; *p* = preposition; *op* = object of the preposition; *prep* = prepositional phrase).

1. With axes, the older boys split the wood into pieces.

2. Inside the family room, the girls built a fire in the fireplace.

Lessons to Practice
Introductory Prepositional Phrases

1. Analyze the following sentences (*S* = subject; *PV* = predicate verb; *hv* = helping verb; *adv* = adverb; *adj* = adjective; *do* = direct object; *p* = preposition; *op* = object of the preposition; *prep* = prepositional phrase).

    a. At school, the children devoured the birthday treat before recess.

    b. Near the playground, some children skipped with jump ropes.

    c. In the muddy fields, the two teams played soccer.

    d. After recess, the children had muddy shoes again.

2. What is an object of the *preposition*?

    ____

    ____

3. Imagine that you are at a basketball game at school. With that in mind, complete the phrase for each preposition listed, and then write a sentence that includes the phrase.

   a. above ______________________________

      Sentence: ______________________________

      ____

   b. under ______________________________

      Sentence: ______________________________

      ____

Lessons to Learn
Introductory Prepositional Phrases

Review It

Practice makes perfect. Can you answer the following questions?

What is a preposition?

What is an object of the preposition?

What is a phrase?

List all of the forty-seven prepositions you have learned.

Learn It

In the following sentences, use the words supplied in the word bank to fill in the missing subject or verb.

Example: In the breeze, the ____________________ waved softly.

Word Bank: scouts, collected, leader, pillow, unfolded, scolded

1. Before the campout, the scouts ____________________ firewood.
2. During dinner, the ____________________ assigned tents.
3. Near the fire, Theo neatly ____________________ campstools.
4. Under the trees, five ____________________ roasted marshmallows.
5. Inside one tent, a ____________________ exploded into a cloud of feathers.

6. Outside that tent, the leader ______________________ the boys.

scolded

Analyze It

Analyze the following sentences (*S* = subject; *PV* = predicate verb; *hv* = helping verb; *adv* = adverb; *adj* = adjective; *do* = direct object; *p* = preposition; *op* = object of the preposition; *prep* = prepositional phrase).

1. Without it, Mom did not know the way.

2. During the tournament, we ate hot dogs with spicy ketchup.

Lessons to Practice

Introductory Prepositional Phrases

B

1. Analyze the following sentences (*S* = subject; *PV* = predicate verb; *hv* = helping verb; *adv* = adverb; *adj* = adjective; *do* = direct object; *p* = preposition; *op* = object of the preposition; *prep* = prepositional phrase).

   a. From the north, the icy winds blew the cedar trees backward.

   b. During the storm, the cousins obediently stayed inside the house.

   c. Throughout the night, the snow flew around the snow fort.

   d. From the window, the children looked at the fresh white carpet.

2. What is a *preposition*?

   ____

   ____

3. Imagine you are spending a snowy day with the cousins (Theo, Peggy, and Lucy) and Stripes. With that in mind, complete the phrase for each preposition listed, and then write a sentence that includes the phrase.

   a. beneath ______________________________

      Sentence: ______________________________

      ____

   b. in ______________________________

      Sentence: ______________________________

      ____

Lessons to Learn
Introductory Prepositional Phrases

Review It

Answer the following questions:

What do prepositions do in a sentence?

What are prepositions?

What is a phrase?

What is an object of the preposition?

Can you think of a sentence with a prepositional phrase following the verb?

Can you rearrange that sentence and make the prepositional phrase introductory?

Learn It

Keep in mind that introductory prepositional phrases are adverbial, so they tell *where* or *when* (and sometimes *how*) the action in the sentence is happening. Fill in the missing preposition in each of the following sentences.

Example: ______Beside______ the river, they collect rocks.

1. ____________________ a cave, Dad found an arrowhead.

2. ____________________ the little waterfall, Mom took pictures.

3. ____________________ a rock, Peggy found a crayfish.

4. ____________________ the red cliffs, Theo saw a bumpy toad.

5. ______________________ several pools, the tadpoles swam.

6. ______________________ lunch, the family drove to the beach.

Analyze It

Analyze the following sentences (*S* = subject; *PV* = predicate verb; *hv* = helping verb; *adv* = adverb; *adj* = adjective; *do* = direct object; *p* = preposition; *op* = object of the preposition; *prep* = prepositional phrase).

1. In the barn, the farmer had three horses.

2. Over the fence, the noisy neighbors talked with the farmer.

Lessons to Practice
Introductory Prepositional Phrases

1. Analyze the following sentences (*S* = subject; *PV* = predicate verb; *hv* = helping verb; *adv* = adverb; *adj* = adjective; *do* = direct object; *p* = preposition; *op* = object of the preposition; *prep* = prepositional phrase).

   a. Beneath a full moon, Grandpa stands with Grandma near a garden wall.

   b. Near the stone bench, Winston held a wooden sword with a shield.

   c. Under the cabbage leaves, a chubby baby lay on a tiny blanket.

   d. During the afternoon, Fritz studied the old pictures for hours.

2. What is an *object of the preposition*?

   ____

   ____

3. Imagine Fritz finding a jellybean jar and knocking it over in the kitchen. With that in mind, complete the phrase for each preposition listed, and then write a sentence that includes the phrase.

   a. on ______________________________

      Sentence: ______________________________

      ____

   b. with ______________________________

      Sentence: ______________________________

      ____

Review It

Answer the following review questions:

What is a preposition?

What is an object of the preposition?

What is a phrase?

Can you list all forty-seven prepositions that you've learned?

Learn It

Play Lightning. Your teacher will say a preposition to a student and ask that student to construct a sentence. The sentence must include the preposition in a phrase placed where the teacher says, either at the beginning of the sentence or after the verb. The student has five seconds to supply a complete sentence that includes the correct form. Then the game moves on to the next student.

Example:

Teacher: "*Between*—introductory."
Student 1: "*Between* you and me, I think spring will be here soon."
Teacher: "*Since*—after the verb."
Student 2: "I have been here *since* Friday."

aboard	about	above	across	after
against	along	among	around	at
before	behind	below	beneath	beside
between	beyond	by	down	during
except	for	from	inside	in
into	near	of	off	on
out	outside	over	past	since
through	throughout	to	toward	under
up	until	upon	with	within
without	underneath			

Lessons to Learn—Review
Introductory Prepositional Phrases

On the lines provided, write your favorite sentence that was created during the game of Lightning.

Lessons to Practice—Review
Introductory Prepositional Phrases

1. Analyze the following sentences: (*S* = subject; *PV* = predicate verb; *hv* = helping verb; *adv* = adverb; *adj* = adjective; *do* = direct object; *p* = preposition; *op* = object of the preposition; *prep* = prepositional phrase).

   a. In the twilight, the family watched from the front window.

   b. Above the wispy clouds, two wild geese flew together in the sky.

   c. Outside the house, Rex barked at a neighbor.

   d. Inside the house, Grandfather read many familiar stories.

2. What is a *preposition*?

   ____

   ____

3. Imagine Peggy and Lucy are listening to Grandpa read. With that in mind, complete the phrase for each preposition listed, and then write a sentence that includes the phrase.

   a. During ______________________________

      Sentence: ______________________________

      ____

   b. After ______________________________

      Sentence: ______________________________

      ____

Lessons to Enjoy—Poem
Introductory Prepositional Phrases

Elves, dwarves, and fairies are delightful imaginary creatures of the forest. In the play *A Midsummer Night's Dream*, William Shakespeare writes this song of a fairy. Another character asks the fairy where she is going, and this poem is her answer. Notice how introductory prepositional phrases are used to tell where she must go to serve her fairy queen.

dale: valley
brier: a tangle of prickly plants
pale: an area that is enclosed, as with a fence
sphere: revolution around the earth
orbs: orbits; a poetic name for the mushrooms called "fairy rings" because they grow in circles as if a fairy had danced there
cowslips: sweet-smelling yellow wildflowers
pensioners: royal attendants, known in Shakespeare's time for being tall and dressed in gold
favors: gifts, as in party favors
savors: sweet smells

Over Hill, Over Dale

by William Shakespeare (1564–1616)

Over hill, over dale,
Through bush, through brier,
Over park, over pale,
Through floor, through fire,
I do wander everywhere,
Swifter than the moon's sphere;
And I serve the fairy queen,
To dew her orbs upon the green.
The cowslips tall her pensioners be:
In their gold coats spots you see;
Those be rubies, fairy favors,
In those freckles live their savors:
I must go seek some dewdrops here
And hang a pearl in every cowslip's ear.[1]

1. William Shakespeare, Act II , Scene 1, "A Wood near Athens," from *A Midsummer Night's Dream* in *World Scope Family Library: Works of William Shakespeare*, ed. W.G. Clark and W.A. Wright (New York: The Universal Guide, Inc., 1950), p. 7.

Questions to Ponder

1. Where does the fairy wander?
2. In the poem, how many introductory prepositional phrases are placed before the first subject and verb?
3. How fast does the fairy travel?
4. What is the fairy's responsibility in the wood?
5. Who guards the fairy queen?

Chapter 5

Compound Subjects

Springtime is a great time to go biking with friends. It is a time when your feet and a pair of wheels determine where you can go and how fast you can get there. Sometimes you are slowly gliding along, and other times you feel like you're actually flying. An English sentence can be like a person on a bike. The subject of the sentence—the noun or pronoun—is the rider, and the predicate is the wheels.

There are many different kinds of bicycles: mountain bikes, racing bikes, BMX (bicycle motocross) bikes; bikes with gears, bikes with baskets, bikes with horns. A fun bike for good friends is a tandem bike, which is built for two or more riders. Can you imagine a sentence that is built for two subjects? Well, we don't call it a tandem sentence, but we do have a name for two subjects for one verb. Both subjects together are referred to as the **compound**■ **subject**. They are joined by a little word, such as *and*, which is called a conjunction. The subjects are the two bicycle riders, the conjunction is the bicycle frame that holds them together, and the predicate is the whole pedaling, wheeling mechanism that moves them along.

To the Source:

■ **compound**

The word *compound* comes from Latin *componere* meaning "to put together."

You see, English sentences can be either bicycles with one rider or bicycles with multiple riders. You can write a sentence about an individual (a singular subject) doing individual activities. Alternatively, you can write a sentence that is like a tandem bike with more than one rider. It has several individuals (a compound subject) doing together the activity expressed in the verb. Strap on your safety helmet. *You and your teacher* (compound subject!) are off for a ride.

Ideas to Understand

When two or more subjects have the same predicate and are joined with a conjunction, they are called a compound subject. A conjunction acts like the glue in a sentence and does not express any distinct idea in itself; it serves to make a clearer connection between ideas. **Conjunctions**■ are one of the eight parts of speech. There are different kinds of conjunctions, and they can join words, phrases, or clauses. You'll learn more about them in *WOL Level 2*. In this chapter, we will focus on only two conjunctions—*and*, *or*—because they are the ones that most often glue nouns or pronouns together to form a compound subject.

To the Source:

■ **conjunction**

In Latin *conjunction* is *conjunction*, which means "connection or joining together."

In the middle of his nonsensical poem "The Walrus and the Carpenter" (you'll find the complete poem in The Curious Child's Literary Appendix), Lewis Carroll tells of two rather strange characters on a beach:

The Walrus and the Carpenter
  Walked on a mile or so,
And then they rested on a rock
  Conveniently low:
And all the little Oysters stood
  And waited in a row.

'The time has come,' the Walrus said,
  'To talk of many things:
Of shoes—and ships—and sealing wax—
  Of cabbages—and kings—
And why the sea is boiling hot—
  And whether pigs have wings.'[1]

Carroll could have written "The Walrus walked on a mile or so" and "The Carpenter walked on a mile or so" as two separate sentences, but instead he combines two subjects, *Walrus* and *Carpenter*, into one sentence using the same verb—*walked*. He connects *Walrus* and *Carpenter* into a compound subject using the conjunction *and*. Notice that the third line quoted above uses the plural subject *they*. It is not a compound but simply a plural pronoun, so there is no conjunction.

1. Lewis Carroll, "The Walrus and the Carpenter," *Through the Looking-Glass* (New York: Random House, 1916), pp. 56–61.

When using a compound subject, you must make sure that the verb agrees with the subject. For most compound subjects joined with *and*, the rule is very simple: use the plural form of the verb.

> The Walrus and the Oysters **talk** of many things.
> The Oysters and the Walrus **talk** of many things.

For compound subjects connected with the conjunction *or*, the rule is a little more complicated. The part of the subject that is closer to the verb dictates the number of the verb (in other words, that's the part that decides whether the verb is singular or plural).

> The Walrus or the Oysters **talk** of many things.
> The Oysters or the Walrus **talks** of many things.

If the plural part of a compound subject with *or* is next to the verb, the verb takes a plural form: *the oysters **talk***. If the singular part of a compound subject with *or* is next to the verb, the verb takes a singular form: *the walrus **talks***.

If the sentence includes helping verbs, then the helping verb—rather than the main verb—follows the rules stated for agreeing in number with the subjects. The agreement of subjects and helping verbs will be explored more fully in later lessons, but here are a few examples of correct helping verb choices based on whether the conjunction in the compound subject is *and* or *or*:

1. The Walrus *and* the Oysters **are** talking of many things.
   Are the Walrus *and* the Oysters talking of many things?
2. The Walrus *or* the Oysters **are** talking of many things.
   Is the Walrus *or* the Oysters talking of many things?
3. The Oysters *or* the Walrus **is** talking of many things.
   Are the Oysters or the Walrus talking of many things?

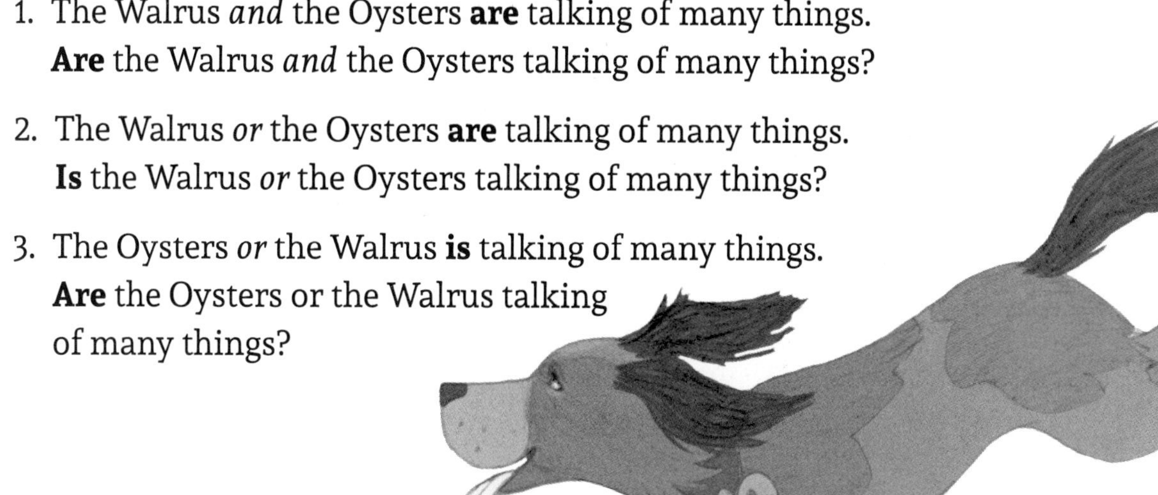

Terms to Remember

It is often said that once you learn how to ride a bike, you never forget. Well, once you memorize these grammar terms, you will know them for life.

Eight Parts of Speech *(1–1)*

The eight parts of speech are classes of words
with the same kind of meaning and use.
They are: nouns, verbs, adjectives, adverbs,
prepositions, pronouns, conjunctions, interjections.
These are the eight parts of speech,
classes of words with the same kind of meaning and use. *(Repeat.)*

Principal Elements *(1–3)*

Principal elements are the parts of the sentence
that are needed for the sentence to be completed.
Subject and predicate are those two parts.

Subject and Predicate *(1–4)*

A subject, a subject is a noun or a pronoun
and is what the sentence is about *(clap, clap).*
A predicate, a predicate tells us something about the subject
like what it is doing or being *(clap, clap).*

Nouns *(1–5)*

A noun is a part of speech.
It names a person, place, or thing.
A noun names a quality or an idea.
A noun is a part of speech.
It names a person, place, or thing.
A noun may be singular *(clap)* or plural *(clap clap clap). (Repeat.)*

NEW! Conjunction *(1–20)*

A conjunction is a part of speech.
It joins elements of the same rank or name.

When two or more words are joined this way, they're called compounds. *(Repeat.)*

Sentences to Analyze

Now that we are studying compound subjects, you need to be on the lookout for conjunctions in a sentence. When you find a conjunction, you will mark it with angle brackets (> <) on either side of the word: Walrus >and< Carpenter. We call the brackets "wings." Before you begin the rest of the analysis, make sure that you mark the conjunctions with wings. Then continue the analysis and mark the sentence using the questions below to help. Say the words in gray together.

S S PV
The Walrus⟩and⟨the Carpenter walked together.
adj adj adv

a. (First, read the sentence aloud.) "The Walrus and the Carpenter walked together."

b. "Are there any conjunctions?" (Choral response: "Yes, sir.") (Since *and* is a conjunction, put wings before and after it.)

c. "The order of analysis is phrases, clauses, principal elements, modifiers."

d. "Are there any prepositional phrases?" (Choral response: "No, sir." Since there are none you can answer *no* and continue.)

e. "This is a sentence and it is declarative."

f. "This sentence is about *Walrus and Carpenter*. So, *Walrus and Carpenter* are the subjects because they are what the sentence is about." (Since *Walrus and Carpenter* are the subjects, underline them and place a capital letter *S* above each subject.)

g. "*And* is the conjunction."

h. "This sentence tells us that Walrus and Carpenter *walked*. So, *walked* is the predicate because it is what the sentence tells us about *Walrus and Carpenter*." (Since *walked* tells us something about Walrus and Carpenter, double underline the predicate and place a capital letter *P* above it.) "It is a predicate verb because it shows action. There is no linking verb because predicate verbs do not need linking verbs." (Since *walked* shows action, place a capital letter *V* to the right of the letter *P* above the predicate.)

i. "*Together* tells us *how* Walrus and Carpenter walked." (Since *together* tells *how* Walrus and Carpenter walked, draw a straight line down from the adverb, then a horizontal line toward the word it modifies, and then a straight line with an arrow pointing to the word it modifies. "So, *together* is an adverbial element because it modifies a verb. It is an adverb." (Write *adv* in lowercase letters in the elbow opposite the line with the arrow.)

j. "*The* is an adjective."[2] (Since *the* tells *which* carpenter, it an adjective. Draw a straight line down from the adjective, then a horizontal line toward the word it modifies, and then a straight line with an arrow pointing to *carpenter*. Write *adj* in lowercase letters in the elbow opposite the line with the arrow.)

k. "*The* is an adjective."[3] (Since *the* tells *which* walrus, it an adjective. Draw a straight line down from the adjective, then a horizontal line toward the word it modifies, and then a straight line with an arrow pointing to *walrus*. Write *adj* in lowercase letters in the elbow opposite the line with the arrow.)

Did you know that there are bicycles that are built for even more than two people? There are even bikes that can be used by five people! Just as there are bicycles that more than two people can ride, a compound subject can contain more than two subjects. The same grammar rules apply no matter how many subjects are contained in the compound.

If ever you have ridden a tandem bicycle, you know that the pedals work in unison, so the riders must move their feet together. They must lean into the turns together. Their tandem seats are connected together on the bicycle frame. So it is with the parts of a compound subject. They are connected together with a conjunction. Together they are what the sentence is about. One verb expresses the action that together they are doing.

---

2. The words *article adjective* can be substituted in place of the word *adjective*.
3. The words *article adjective* can be substituted in place of the word *adjective*.

Notes

Introductory Lesson
Compound Subjects

Review It

You have learned a lot of grammar terms so far. Can you answer these questions without checking?

What are the eight parts of speech?

What are principal elements?

What are nouns?

What is a conjunction?

Learn It

Remember that if the compound subject is joined by the word *and*, it is considered plural because there are two subjects. Since verbs must agree with their subjects, pay careful attention to both. Fill in the missing verbs in the sentences below.

Example: Lucy *and* Fritz usually _____climb_____ on the jungle gym.

1. Theo and Winston __________________ to the park.

2. Peggy and you __________________ bringing the water bottles later.

3. Heidi and I __________________ the soccer equipment.

4. Uncle Ulysses and the boys __________________ coming to the game too.

Analyze It

Analyze the following sentences (*S* = subject; *PV* = predicate verb; *hv* = helping verb; *adv* = adverb; *adj* = adjective; *do* = direct object; *p* = preposition; *op* = object of the preposition; *prep* = prepositional phrase).

1. You and I can surprise the cousins with water balloons.

2. Did Uncle Ulysses or Theo put the balloons in the crate?

Introductory Practice
Compound Subjects

1. Analyze the following sentences (*S* = subject; *PV* = predicate verb; *hv* = helping verb; *adv* = adverb; *adj* = adjective; *do* = direct object; *p* = preposition; *op* = object of the preposition; *prep* = prepositional phrase).

   a. On Tuesday, Peggy and I went with the family to the library.

   b. Did you and Dad get pirate books?

   c. Theo and Lucy should not have been running around the tables.

   d. Afterward Dad and the group headed to the market.

2. Complete the following sentences by adding a verb after the compound subject. You may also add a direct object, an adverb, or a prepositional phrase to construct each sentence.

   a. In the library, will Mr. Michaels and you ______________________________

   ____?

   b. Yesterday Heidi and Peggy ______________________________

   ____.

c. Later Theo and two boys ____

____.

3. Imagine that you see Lucy at the library. With that in mind, write a sentence about it, being sure to include a compound subject.

____

____

Lessons to Learn
Compound Subjects

Review It

What is a conjunction?

Give an example of a sentence with the conjunction *and*.

Give an example of a sentence with the conjunction *or*.

Learn It

Remember, if a compound subject is joined by the word *or*, it can be either singular or plural depending on the subject that is closer to the verb. The verb must agree in number with the closer subject.

Example: Winston *or* the boys (is playing / are playing) basketball tonight.

The boys *or* Winston (is playing / are playing) basketball tonight.

Circle the correct verb that goes with the compound subject in each of the following sentences.

1. The neighbors or Grandpa Fred often (drives / drive) the kids.
2. Lucy or Theo (is coming / are coming) to the movies with us too.
3. Usually Fritz or the other boys (sits / sit) in the backseat.
4. Peggy or all the girls (is asking / are asking) for popcorn.
5. The aunts or just Grandma Lola (is meeting / are meeting) us there.

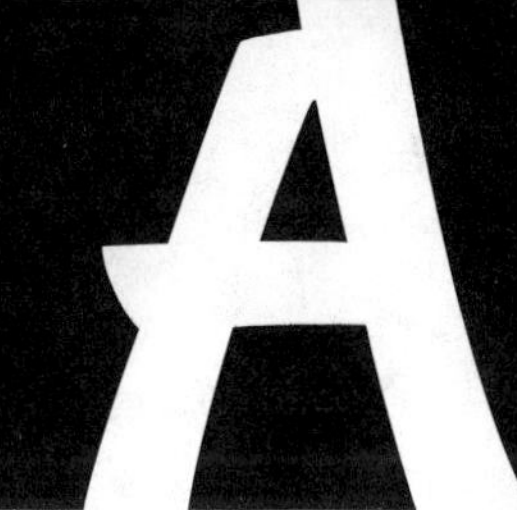

Lessons to Learn
Compound Subjects

Analyze It

Analyze the following sentences (*S* = subject; *PV* = predicate verb; *hv* = helping verb; *adv* = adverb; *adj* = adjective; *do* = direct object; *p* = preposition; *op* = object of the preposition; *prep* = prepositional phrase).

1. Will the green knight or the white knight win the battle?

2. During the tournament, the queen and the princess return.

Lessons to Practice

Compound Subjects

1. Analyze the following sentences (*S* = subject; *PV* = predicate verb; *hv* = helping verb; *adv* = adverb; *adj* = adjective; *do* = direct object; *p* = preposition; *op* = object of the preposition; *prep* = prepositional phrase).

   a. Near the forest, the turtle and the rabbit have a race.

   b. The sly fox and the brown hedgehog wait for the turtle.

   c. Slowly the turtle crawls along the path.

   d. At the end, does the turtle or the rabbit learn the lesson?

2. Complete the following sentences by adding a verb after the compound subject. You may also add a direct object, an adverb, or a prepositional phrase to construct each sentence.

   a. Grandma and Grandpa ______________________________

   ______________________________.

b. Will Mom or the girls ____

____?

c. Fritz and Lucy ____

____.

3. Imagine there is a hedgehog at the race between the turtle and the rabbit. With that in mind, write a sentence about it, being sure to include a compound subject.

____

____

Lessons to Learn
Compound Subjects

Review It

Can you answer the following questions by heart?

What are the eight parts of speech?

What are principal elements?

What are nouns?

What is a conjunction?

Learn It

What happens to the predicate in a sentence when another subject is added? If the sentence has a compound subject that includes the conjunction *and*, then it is plural and the verb should agree with it. In the following sentences, add the conjunction *and* along with another subject to form a compound subject. Then, change the verb so it agrees with the compound subject. Write each new sentence on the lines provided.

Example: The robin sings in the morning.
The robin *and the blackbird sing* in the morning.

1. Stripes hides under the porch. ______________________________

____

2. Slowly Fritz brings the four buckets to the truck. ______________

____

3. Heidi washes the car in the afternoon. ______________________

____

4. Dad surprises the kids with Popsicles. ______________________________

____

Analyze It

Analyze the following sentences (*S* = subject; *PV* = predicate verb; *hv* = helping verb; *adv* = adverb; *adj* = adjective; *do* = direct object; *p* = preposition; *op* = object of the preposition; *prep* = prepositional phrase).

1. The younger brother and the older sister raced toward the red line.

2. Will you or I award the winners?

Lessons to Practice

Compound Subjects

B

1. Analyze the following sentences (*S* = subject; *PV* = predicate verb; *hv* = helping verb; *adv* = adverb; *adj* = adjective; *do* = direct object; *p* = preposition; *op* = object of the preposition; *prep* = prepositional phrase).

   a. The harsh winds and the icy rain pelted against the window.

   b. Will Coach Stevens or Coach Howard cancel soccer practice tonight?

   c. Mom and the kids were hoping for the phone call.

   d. Reluctantly Heidi and Fritz climbed into the van for practice.

2. Add compound subjects to the sentences below.

   a. ______________________________ race cars.

   b. ______________________________ fly kites.

   c. ______________________________ will climb trees.

   d. ______________________________ explore.

3. Imagine the soccer team is on the field in the rain. With that in mind, write a sentence about it, being sure to include a compound subject.

____

____

Lessons to Learn
Compound Subjects

Review It

List the eight parts of speech on a sheet of paper. See if you can define from memory the seven parts of speech that you have learned. (You don't have to define an interjection yet. You'll learn that definition in *Well-Ordered Language Level 2*.)

Learn It

Subtract a subject and the conjunction from the following sentences and rewrite them on the lines provided. You might have to change the verb to make it agree with the subject.

Example: *Winston and Theo play* basketball in the outside court.
**   *Winston plays* basketball in the outside court.**

1. Peggy and Heidi eat potato chips on a bench nearby.

____

____

2. Does that water bottle or the thermos have a leak?

____

____

3. Lucy and Fritz watch silently at the park.

____

____

4. Will Dad or Mom come for the kids at noon?

____

____

Analyze It

Analyze the following sentences (*S* = subject; *PV* = predicate verb; *hv* = helping verb; *adv* = adverb; *adj* = adjective; *do* = direct object; *p* = preposition; *op* = object of the preposition; *prep* = prepositional phrase).

1. In the forest, Olive Tree and Fig Tree serve others.

2. Will Vine or Thornbush reign over the trees?

Lessons to Practice

Compound Subjects

1. Analyze the following sentences (*S* = subject; *PV* = predicate verb; *hv* = helping verb; *adv* = adverb; *adj* = adjective; *do* = direct object; *p* = preposition; *op* = object of the preposition; *prep* = prepositional phrase).

   a. Dad and the girls planned a trip to the butterfly exhibit.

   b. Peggy and Lucy love bright butterflies.

   c. Can Heidi or Fritz come along on the trip?

   d. Later, among the branches, the girls saw beautiful butterflies.

2. Complete the following sentences by adding a verb after the compound subject. You may also add a direct object, an adverb, or a prepositional phrase to construct each sentence.

   a. The guitarist and drummer ______________________________

   ______________________________.

   b. Lucy and Fritz ______________________________

   ______________________________.

c. Later, the lady singer and the piano player ______________________________

____.

3. Imagine Winston, Heidi, and Fritz are going to a concert with their parents. With that in mind, write a sentence about it, being sure to use a compound subject.

____

____

Review It

Answer the following review questions:

What is a preposition?

What is an object of the preposition?

What is a phrase?

Can you list all of the forty-seven prepositions you've learned?

Learn It

Play Lightning to form sentences with compound subjects. Your teacher will give a topic to the first student, who will say two nouns. The second student will construct a sentence using the two nouns (compound subject).

Example: Teacher: "Two rivers."
Student 1: "The Mississippi River and the Missouri River."
Student 2: "The Mississippi River and the Missouri River are major water highways."

Two pets people keep

Two players on a team

Two places your family visits

Two days of the week

Two toys you play with

Two books in your room

Two states bordering an ocean

Two months of the year

Two boys in your class

Two creatures in the forest

Two fruits you eat

Two games you play

Two foods you eat for lunch

Two people in your family

Two authors of books

Two people who sit near you

Two animals in a zoo

Two girls in your neighborhood

Two people you visit

Lessons to Practice—Review

Compound Subjects

1. Analyze the following sentences: (*S* = subject; *PV* = predicate verb; *hv* = helping verb; *adv* = adverb; *adj* = adjective; *do* = direct object; *p* = preposition; *op* = object of the preposition; *prep* = prepositional phrase).

   a. On Monday, Mom and I will be working at the food shelter.

   b. Several men and women stood in line outside.

   c. Did she or you shovel the sidewalks for the people?

   d. Foolishly many children and toddlers raced about at the shelter.

2. Complete the following sentences by adding a verb after the compound subject. You may also add a direct object, an adverb, or a prepositional phrase to construct each sentence.

   a. In science class, Heidi and Peggy ______________________________

   ______________________________.

b. Can a parrot or a toucan ____

____?

c. The teacher and the students ____

____.

3. Imagine you are on a field trip at the zoo and you're standing in the bird room. With that in mind, write a sentence, being sure to use a compound subject.

____

____

Notes

Have you heard the saying "Be careful what you wish because you might get it"? Sometimes we are so sure we want something that we think we *must* have it no matter what. However, when we get it, we may end up regretting it. In this Hebrew fable, the forest trees decide they want a king to rule over them, so they ask an olive tree, a fig tree, a vine, and a thornbush each to be their leader. Which one will agree to be the leader, and will they be happy with their new king at the end?

The Trees Choose a King

Hebrew Fable

anoint: apply oil in a special ceremony

hold sway over: rule over

Cedars of Lebanon: in the ancient world, this vast forest of cedar trees in the country of Lebanon supplied wood for many structures, ships, and religious ceremonies in various cultures

One day, the Trees went out to anoint a King for themselves. They said to the Olive Tree, "Be our King."

But the Olive Tree answered, "Should I give up my oil, by which both gods and men are honored, to hold sway over the Trees?"

Next, the Trees said to the Fig Tree, "Come and be our King."

But the Fig Tree replied, "Should I give up my fruit, so good and sweet, to hold sway over the Trees?"

Then the Trees said to the [Grape] Vine, "Come and be our King."

But the Vine answered, "Should I give up my wine, which cheers both gods and men, to hold sway over the Trees?"

Finally, the Trees said to the Thornbush, "Come and be our King."

The Thornbush said to the Trees, "If you really want to anoint me King over you, come and take refuge in my shade; but if not, then let fire come out of the Thornbush and consume the Cedars of Lebanon!"

Moral: May your mouth match the intentions of your heart.[1]

Questions to Ponder

1. Why do you think the Trees wanted to anoint a King for themselves?
2. What Trees are named in the fable?
3. Can you tell in your own words what the Thornbush says to the Trees?

1. "The Trees Choose a King," taken from *Writing & Rhetoric Book 1: Fable* by Paul Kortepeter (Camp Hill, PA: Classical Academic Press, 2013), p. 115.

Chapter 6

Compound Verbs

When you think of a thunderstorm, flashes of lightning and booms of thunder are probably the first things that come to your mind. Did you know that lightning and thunder actually happen at the same time? A bolt of lightning, which is more than 40,000 degrees Fahrenheit, heats the air around it, causing the air to expand quickly. Thunder is the result of the rapid expanding and contracting of the atmosphere that is caused by the bolt of lightning. The two events happen at the same time, but light travels faster than sound (in other words, you see the lightning before you hear the thunder).

In an English sentence, when one thing (a subject) does two or more actions (has two verbs), those actions are called a **compound verb**. Sometimes writers use many subjects with only one verb (a compound subject), and sometimes writers use one subject with many verbs (a compound verb). Either way, the compound elements are joined together with conjunctions. A compound verb gives you the power to describe vividly with multiple action words that midnight storm that once woke you up with a jolt: "The terrible tempest *flashed and rumbled.*"

Ideas to Understand

When two or more verbs are joined with a conjunction and have the same subject, they are called a compound verb. In Rudyard Kipling's story "How the Whale Got His Throat," two verbs—*swam* and *swam*—are joined with a conjunction, *and*. Together they form a compound verb:

Off the Shelf: Kipling's Whale is swimming and swimming to a precise location on the globe that is indicated by "latitude" and "longitude." Have you ever noticed the parallel lines on a globe, including the equator, that are drawn horizontally? They are lines of latitude. The vertical lines that are drawn between the North and South Poles are called longitude. Can you find latitude 50 North, longitude 40 West on a globe? That's where the Whale swam and swam.

> So the Whale swam and swam to latitude Fifty North, longitude Forty West, as fast as he could swim and *on* a raft, *in* the middle of the sea, *with* nothing to wear except a pair of blue canvas breeches, a pair of suspenders (you must particularly remember the suspenders, Best Beloved), *and* a jack-knife, he found one single, solitary shipwrecked Mariner, trailing his toes in the water.[1]

Kipling doubles his verbs and uses a long sentence to demonstrate the great distance the Whale swam. He didn't just swim; he *swam* ***and*** *swam*. Kipling's compound verb is unusual because it is the same word repeated twice. Compound verbs are often two different verbs or even more than two verbs. In the sentence "The whales swam, dove, and fished," the subject is *whales*, and three verbs—*swam*, *dove*, and *fished*—connected by a conjunction form the compound verb.

Just as in any other sentence, subjects and compound verbs must agree in number. A whale swims and swims, but whales swim and swim. The singular subject *whale* agrees with singular verbs, *swims* and *swims*. The plural subject *whales* agrees with plural verbs, *swim* and *swim*.

The verbs in a compound verb also can be separated by more than just a conjunction. Sometimes a direct object or even a prepositional phrase can separate the verbs. Take a look at the following examples:

With a ***conjunction***:

The whale *swims* >and< *spurts* water.

With a ***direct object*** and ***conjunction***:

The whale *spurts* water >and< *splashes* the dolphins.

With a ***direct object***, ***conjunction***, and ***prepositional phrase***:

The whale *spurts* water into the air >and< *splashes* the dolphins nearby.

A compound verb can include helping verbs too. If the compound verb includes only one helping verb, there is an implied helping verb for the second verb. For instance, consider the following sentence: "The whale is swimming and spurting water." The helping verb *is* assists both verbs to complete their meaning. The author is really saying that the whale *is swimming* >and< *is spurting* water, but the helping verb does not need to be repeated.

1. Rudyard Kipling, "How the Whale Got His Throat," *Just So Stories* (New York: Doubleday, CO, 1952), p. 9.

Terms to Remember

Since there are only a couple of definitions to practice for this chapter, now is a good time to add an important concept to memorize. Do you already know what **synonyms**, **antonyms**, and **homonyms** are? In this chapter, knowing synonyms will come in handy for a few of the lessons. Remember, a synonym is a word that means almost the same thing as another word. For example, a synonym for *ocean* is *sea*.

Verbs and Helping Verbs *(1–6)*

A verb is a part of speech. *(echo)*
A verb shows action or a state of being. *(echo)*
A verb is a part of speech. *(echo)*
A verb shows action or a state of being. *(echo)*
A helping verb helps another verb to express its meaning.
A helping verb stands near the verb.
It is called an auxiliary.
Am, is, are, was, were, be, being, been, has, have, had, do, does, did, may, might, must, should, could, would, shall, will, and *can.*
A helping verb stands near the verb and is called an auxiliary.
A helping verb stands near the verb. It is called an auxiliary.

Conjunction *(1–20)*

A conjunction is a part of speech.
It joins elements of the same rank or name.
When two or more words are joined this way, they're called compounds. *(Repeat.)*

NEW! Synonyms, Antonyms, and Homonyms *(1–21)*

Synonyms, antonyms, and homonyms
Synonyms are words that mean almost the same thing.
Antonyms are words that have the opposite meaning.
Homonyms are words that sound the same, but have different meaning and sometimes spelling—words that sound the same, but do not mean the same thing.
Synonyms, antonyms, and homonyms
Synonyms: little and small

Antonyms: short and tall
Homonyms: threw the ball, walk through the mall
Synonyms, antonyms, and homonyms
Synonyms, antonyms, and homonyms.

Sentences to Analyze

As you learned in chapter 5, when you are studying sentences that contain compounds, you need to be on the lookout for conjunctions. Conjunctions are marked with two angle brackets, or "wings," on either side of the word: swam >and< splashed. Before you begin your complete analysis of a sentence, make sure that you mark the conjunctions with wings. The questions that have been added to your analysis script are there to help you analyze the sentence.

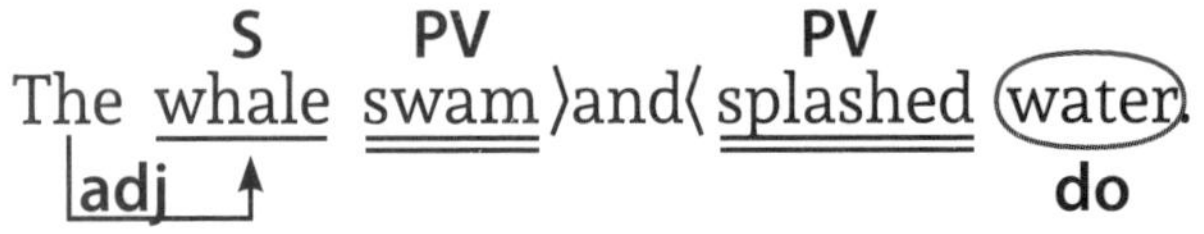

S PV PV
The whale swam ⟩and⟨ splashed water
adj do

a. (First, read the sentence aloud.) "The whale swam and splashed water."

b. "Are there any conjunctions? (Choral response: "Yes, sir.") (Since *and* is a conjunction, put wings before and after it.)

c. "The order of analysis is phrases, clauses, principal elements, modifiers."

d. "Are there any prepositional phrases?" (Since there are none, you can answer *no* and continue.)

e. "This is a sentence, and it is declarative."

f. "This sentence is about *whale*. So, *whale* is the subject because it is what the sentence is about." (Since *whale* is the subject, underline it and place a capital letter *S* above it.)

g. "This sentence tells us that whale *swam* and *splashed*. So, *swam* and *splashed* are the predicates because they are what the sentence tells us about *whale*." (Since *swam* and *splashed* tell something about whale, double underline the predicates and place a capital letter *P* above each of them.) "They are predicate verbs because they show action. There is no linking verb because predicate verbs do not need linking verbs." (Since *swam* and *splashed* both show action, place a capital letter *V* to the right of the letter *P* above each predicate.)

h. "*And* is the conjunction."

i. "*Water* tells us what whale swam and splashed." (Since *water* tells *what* whale swam and splashed, draw a circle around it.) "So, *water* is an objective element because it completes the meaning of an action verb. It is a direct object because it tells *what* whale swam and splashed." (Write *do* in lowercase letters beneath the direct object.)

j. "*The* is an adjective."[2] (Since *the* is an adjective, draw a straight line down from the adjective, then a horizontal line toward the word that it modifies, and then a straight line with an arrow pointing to the word it modifies. Write *adj* in lowercase letters in the elbow opposite the line with the arrow.)

Do you remember our vivid sentence about the thunderstorm? "The terrible tempest *flashed and rumbled.*" Using a compound verb made the scene described in the sentence easier to imagine. Now let's take that same sentence and apply some of the other things you are learning in this chapter. Let's choose different verbs and add direct objects and prepositional phrases: "The terrible tempest *shook* my bedroom in the middle of the night *and rattled* the trophies on my shelf." Adding a helping verb to a compound verb can make the action exciting and immediate, like this: "The thunderstorm *is terrifying* Rex *and keeping* me awake!" The words that you choose as a writer and where you place them in the sentence help you express your ideas in lively ways.

2. The words *article adjective* can be substituted in place of the word *adjective*.

Introductory Lesson
Compound Verbs

Review It

What is a verb? Can you think of five verbs? Can you add helping verbs to the verbs? Can you add another verb to each of your original five verbs? What is a synonym? Can you think of a synonym for *jump*?

Learn It

How does a sentence change when another verb is added to it? Using the following sentences, construct new sentences by adding a conjunction (*and*, *or*) and another verb to form compound verbs.

Example: The new season came _____*and changed*_____ the prairie.

1. The spring birds chirped ______________________________

   to one another.

2. Joyously the flowers grew ______________________________ .

3. On April 6, a storm drenched ______________________________

   the ground.

4. In the garden, the crocus flowers wilted ____________________ .

Analyze It

Analyze the following sentences (*S* = subject; *PV* = predicate verb; *hv* = helping verb; *adv* = adverb; *adj* = adjective; *do* = direct object; *p* = preposition; *op* = object of the preposition; *prep* = prepositional phrase).

1. Outside the tent, Lucy watched and pondered the distant stars.

2. Under the night sky, Theo stretched and yawned loudly.

Introductory Practice
Compound Verbs

1. Analyze the following sentences (*S* = subject; *PV* = predicate verb; *hv* = helping verb; *adv* = adverb; *adj* = adjective; *do* = direct object; *p* = preposition; *op* = object of the preposition; *prep* = prepositional phrase).

   a. Four girls wrapped and stacked the birthday gifts.

   b. The older boys swept and cleaned the den for the party.

   c. Aunt Gabby baked and decorated a birthday cake for them.

   d. Suddenly Mom and Dad surprised us with ice cream.

2. Imagine how different people and animals *walk*. With that in mind, write the following sentences using synonyms for the word *walk*.

   a. Write a sentence about a *girl walking*.

   ____

   ____

b. Write a sentence about a *poodle walking.*

____

____

c. Write a sentence about a *scientist walking.*

____

____

Lessons to Learn
Compound Verbs

To the Source:

■ **review**

Review is from the Latin word *revidere,* from *re-* "again" + *videre* "to see," hence "to see again." The sense of the word is the "process of going over something again."

Review It

To *review*■ something means you are to look back on or keep thinking about something. Review the following grammar terms.

Verbs

Helping verbs

Compound verbs

Conjunctions

Synonym

Antonyms

Homonyms

Learn It

Using the following sentences, construct new sentences by adding a conjunction (*and*, *or*) and another verb to form compound verbs.

Example: Earlier Mom drove __and listened to__ the kids before the game.

1. Does the team often practice ______________________________ in the sleet?

2. Both girls shivered ______________________________ in the cold during the soccer game.

3. The white snow fell ______________________________ the field.

4. Heidi dribbled ________________________________

   the ball down the field.

5. Suddenly the parents shouted ________________________

   for another goal.

Analyze It

Analyze the following sentences (*S* = subject; *PV* = predicate verb; *hv* = helping verb; *adv* = adverb; *adj* = adjective; *do* = direct object; *p* = preposition; *op* = object of the preposition; *prep* = prepositional phrase).

1. Should we ride bikes or walk together to the picnic?

2. Afterward the cousins played games and romped outside.

Lessons to Practice
Compound Verbs

1. Analyze the following sentences (*S* = subject; *PV* = predicate verb; *hv* = helping verb; *adv* = adverb; *adj* = adjective; *do* = direct object; *p* = preposition; *op* = object of the preposition; *prep* = prepositional phrase).

   a. Winston sorted and counted the stamps.

   b. He should have kept and cherished the rare stamp book.

   c. Grandpa Fred carefully cut and sealed each envelope for him.

   d. After lunch, Fritz came and watched the two stamp collectors.

2. Imagine how different people *talk*. With that in mind, write the following sentences using synonyms for the word *talk*.

   a. Write a sentence about a *librarian talking*.

   ____

   ____

b. Write a sentence about a *coach talking.*

____

____

c. Write a sentence about a *grumpy old man talking.*

____

____

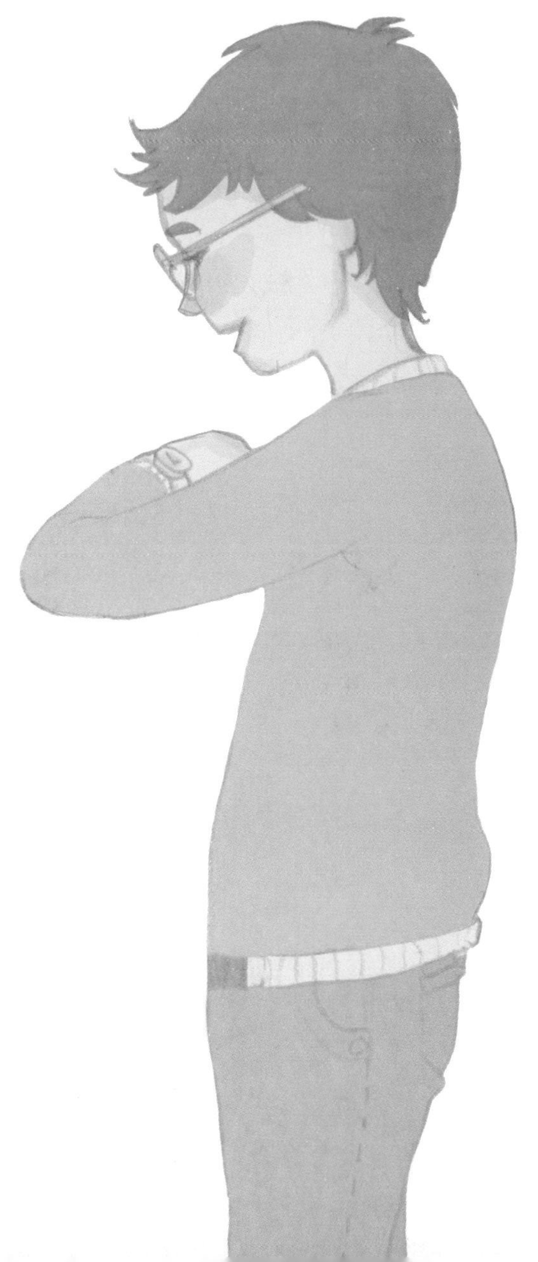

Lessons to Learn
Compound Verbs

Review It

Recitation (repeating something aloud) is a part of good learning. You will remember for your whole life these important definitions you're learning in the Well-Ordered Language series. See how well you can answer the following questions from memory: What is a verb? Can you name the twenty-three helping verbs? What is a conjunction? What is a synonym? What is an antonym? What is a homonym?

Learn It

As you work in teams of three students, your teacher will guide you to add words to the following sentences to construct more descriptive sentences.

Example: "The tadpole swims."
Teacher: "Add another verb."
Student 1: "The tadpole swims *and dives*."
Teacher: "Add an adjective."
Student 2: "The *frisky* tadpole swims and dives."
Teacher: "Add a prepositional phrase."
Student 3: "The frisky tadpole swims and dives *in the shallow pool*."

1. The monkeys reached.

____

____

2. The chimpanzees ran.

____

____

3. Are those apes dancing?

____

____

4. That zookeeper laughed.

____

____

5. Write your favorite newly constructed sentence below.

____

____

Analyze It

Analyze the following sentences (*S* = subject; *PV* = predicate verb; *hv* = helping verb; *adv* = adverb; *adj* = adjective; *do* = direct object; *p* = preposition; *op* = object of the preposition; *prep* = prepositional phrase).

1. The younger girls twirled in circles and skipped around.

2. Heidi laughed at the little girls and joined them in the dance.

Lessons to Practice
Compound Verbs

B

1. Analyze the following sentences (*S* = subject; *PV* = predicate verb; *hv* = helping verb; *adv* = adverb; *adj* = adjective; *do* = direct object; *p* = preposition; *op* = object of the preposition; *prep* = prepositional phrase).

   a. Coach Howard talked to the team and encouraged them before warm-ups.

   b. For hours, the team dribbled and passed the basketball.

   c. Patiently he taught the boys and drilled them on new plays.

   d. Did Theo help or cripple the team during the practice?

2. Imagine how different people *hold* things. With that in mind, write the following sentences using synonyms for the word *hold*.

   a. Write a sentence about a *waitress holding* something.

   ____

   ____

b. Write a sentence about a *musician holding* something.

____

____

c. Write a sentence about a *football player holding* something.

____

____

Lessons to Learn
Compound Verbs

Review It

You have learned a great deal about verbs. Let's review some of it.

Can you think of ten verbs?

Can you think of ten helping verbs?

Can you make compound verbs by adding another verb to each of the verbs you came up with?

What is a synonym for *happy*? What is an antonym for *happy*?

Learn It

Fill in compound verbs to complete the following sentences.

Example: We will ___wash and dry___ the clothes for the trip to Wyoming.

1. The cowboys ______________________________
   the cattle to the barn.

2. Grandpa ______________________________
   the children to dinner.

3. The cattle were ______________________________.

4. Fritz ______________________________
   the ranch dog.

Analyze It

Analyze the following sentences (*S* = subject; *PV* = predicate verb; *hv* = helping verb; *adv* = adverb; *adj* = adjective; *do* = direct object; *p* = preposition; *op* = object of the preposition; *prep* = prepositional phrase).

1. The grasshopper played and danced throughout the summer months.

2. The ant busily worked and gathered food for winter.

Lessons to Practice
Compound Verbs

1. Analyze the following sentences (*S* = subject; *PV* = predicate verb; *hv* = helping verb; *adv* = adverb; *adj* = adjective; *do* = direct object; *p* = preposition; *op* = object of the preposition; *prep* = prepositional phrase).

   a. In the bushes, Lucy made a fort and played alone.

   b. Suddenly she cried loudly and ran to the house.

   c. Later during the appointment, she itched and scratched the red bumps.

   d. Anxiously Mom sat and waited with Lucy for the doctor.

2. Imagine how different people and animals run. With that in mind, write the following sentences, being sure to use synonyms for the word *run*.

   a. Write a sentence about *kindergartners running*, but use a synonym for *run*.

   ____

   ____

b. Write a sentence about a *dog running*, but use another synonym for *run*.

____

____

c. Write a sentence about a *gymnast running*, but use another synonym for *run*.

____

____

Review It

Answer the following questions:

What is a verb?

Can you list twenty-three helping verbs?

What is conjunction?

What is a synonym?

What is an antonym?

What are homonyms?

Learn It

Putting words together to make sentences requires a lot of thought, and constructing good sentences requires careful selection of words. For this exercise, you'll use one of the following verbs or choose a card from the "verb jar." Think of a second verb, join the verbs with a conjunction, and construct a sentence using the compound verb you create. See how many sentences you can construct with compound verbs in this way. Can you think of a few with compound subjects too?

Example: *tickles*
Student: (adds verb) ***scratches***
Student (rephrase): "Grandpa ***tickles*** **and** ***scratches*** **Rex under his ear."**

flops	gardens	tramps	sprints	throws
blows	swims	cracks	scrubs	hides
drops	circles	cries	wrestles	limps
slides	crouches	lifts	scurries	hammers

Lessons to Practice—Review
Compound Verbs

1. Analyze the following sentences: (*S* = subject; *PV* = predicate verb; *hv* = helping verb; *adv* = adverb; *adj* = adjective; *do* = direct object; *p* = preposition; *op* = object of the preposition; *prep* = prepositional phrase).

   a. Theo held the cardboard box and peeked at the little creature.

   b. Inside the box, a tiny rabbit huddled and slept under the blanket.

   c. Underneath the steps, two chipmunks burrow tunnels and store nuts.

   d. The furry squirrel climbed trees and chattered loudly at them.

2. Imagine how different people *throw* things. With that in mind, write the following sentences, being sure to use synonyms for the word *throw*.

   a. Write a sentence about a *bride throwing* something, but use a synonym for throw.

   ____

   ____

b. Write a sentence about a *garbage man throwing* something, but use another synonym for throw.

____

____

c. Write a sentence about a *baseball player throwing* a ball, but use another synonym for throw.

____

____

Notes

Lessons to Enjoy—Poem
Compound Verbs

Christina Rossetti was a nineteenth-century English poet who grew up in London and probably spent her holidays at the beach. Her poem "I Dug and Dug Amongst the Snow" contrasts digging in snow with digging in sand. Why do you think she may have written this poem?

I Dug and Dug Amongst the Snow

by Christina Rossetti (1830–1894)

I dug and dug amongst the snow,
And thought the flowers would never grow;
I dug and dug amongst the sand,
And still no green thing came to hand.

Melt, O snow! the warm winds blow
To thaw the flowers and melt the snow;
But all the winds from every land
Will rear no blossom from the sand.[1]

Questions to Ponder

1. What did the poet think about the flowers in winter?
2. What does it mean that "no green thing came to hand"?
3. Is the poem hopeful or sad?

1. Christina Rossetti, "I Dug and Dug Amongst the Snow" from *Illustrated Poems and Songs for Young People*, ed. Mrs. Lucy Sale Barker (London: George Routledge and Sons, 1885), p. 242. Available at: https://books.google.com/books?id=c4ubK21PVw4C.

Notes

Chapter 7

Compound Direct Objects

Perhaps you have heard the saying "less is more." If you shake too much salt on your french fries, then all you taste is the salt. Less salt means more french fry flavor. When creating or designing something, people often apply the idea of "less is more" so they can keep their creation from being too frilly or fancy. Authors apply "less is more" when writing well-crafted sentences. The idea is that using fewer well-chosen words is more effective than using too many words.

Authors often use compound subjects and compound verbs to minimize the number of words they use and thus maximize (make the most of) the effect of the words. In this chapter, you will learn about another way to do this: using **compound direct objects**. Using them allows you to combine short, choppy sentences into one longer, smoother sentence. Your fries could get cold by the time you say, "Please pass the ketchup. Please pass the salt." Try instead, "Please pass the ketchup and the salt."

Ideas to Understand

When a single transitive verb has more than one direct object connected with a conjunction, those direct objects are called a compound direct object. In the poem "A Good Play," the speaker uses this sentence structure as he remembers playing when he was a child with his friend Tom. Can you find the compound direct object?

We built a ship upon the stairs,
All made of back-bedroom chairs,
And filled it full of sofa pillows

To go a-sailing on the billows.
We took a saw and several nails,
And water in the nursery pails;
And Tom said, "Let us also take
An apple and a slice of cake";—
Which was enough for Tom and me
To go a-sailing on, till tea.[1]

tea: for the British, any meal eaten in the late afternoon or early evening

In the second stanza, Stevenson uses three nouns as a compound direct object: *saw*, *nails*, and *water*. All three complete the action of the same verb, *took*: "We took a saw and several nails and water in the nursery pails." He did not write, "We took a saw. We took several nails. We took water in the nursery pails." Why write three sentences to accomplish what he could do in one? Less is more.

Keep in mind that sometimes a sentence may contain two or more direct objects that are not a compound direct object. For instance, Stevenson's sentence, "We built a ship upon the stairs . . . and filled it full of sofa pillows," contains the two direct objects *ship* and *it*. However, they are not a compound because they complete the action of two separate verbs: *built* and *filled*. There is one subject, *we*; a compound verb, *built* and *filled*; and a separate direct object for each verb. *Built* what? A *ship*. *Filled* what? *It*. In that sentence the compound element is the two verbs, not the direct objects. In other words, the poet is really saying, "We built a ship. We filled it." Remember, compound direct objects always share the same verb, like this: We *built* a ship and a dock.

Unfortunately when using pronouns as compound direct objects, many people mistakenly choose subject pronouns instead of object pronouns. This is a problem. Notice in the two examples below how the mix-up can occur.

Incorrect: Mom called **Tom** >**and**< **I** for tea.

Correct: Mom called **Tom** >**and**< **me** for tea.

Incorrect: Did Dad want **Tom** >**or**< **I** to help?

Correct: Did Dad want **Tom** >**or**< **me** to help?

An easy way to check to see if you have the right pronoun when using a compound direct object is to drop the first pronoun, leaving the second

1. Robert Louis Stevenson, "A Good Play," from *Favorite Poems Old and New*, ed. Helen Ferris (New York: Doubleday & Company, Inc., 1957), pp. 101–102.

one to test it. Ask yourself if the remaining pronoun is an object pronoun. In other words, for the examples above, in your mind you would remove *Tom* to test the correctness of the pronoun *I*. You wouldn't say, "Mom called *I* for tea"; you would say, "Mom called *me*." The subject pronoun *I* is clearly the wrong choice, so "Mom called Tom and *me* for tea" is correct. "Did Dad want *I* to help?" No! He wanted *me* to help, so the object pronoun is the correct choice: "Did Dad want Tom or *me* to help?"

Do you have the object pronouns committed to memory? Here's a familiar chart to use for review.

Object Pronouns

	Singular	Plural
First Person	me	us
Second Person	you	you
Third Person	him, her, it	them

Terms to Remember

Here you are at the last chapter of the book, and there are no new terms to memorize. Reviewing these four definitions will help you analyze and write sentences with compound direct objects, using fewer words to say more.

Direct Object *(1–9)*

d-o, d-o
A direct object is an objective element
that tells what the subject is acting on.
d-o, d-o
It's a noun or pronoun after a transitive verb.
d-o, d-o
It answers the question *what* or *whom* after the verb
and is labeled *do*.

Four Classes of Verbs *(1–10)*

These are the four classes of verbs:
The four classes of verbs are transitive verbs, linking verbs,
intransitive verbs, and helping verbs.
These are the four classes of verbs.
A transitive verb takes an objective element.
A linking verb joins a subject to a predicate.
An intransitive verb does not take an objective element
or join a subject to a predicate.
A helping verb helps another verb express its meaning.
A helping verb helps another verb express its meaning.
These are the four classes of verbs.
These are the four classes of verbs.

Conjunction *(1–20)*

A conjunction is a part of speech.
It joins elements of the same rank or name.
When two or more words are joined this way,
they're called compounds. *(Repeat.)*

Object Pronouns *(1–15)*

Object pronouns are in the objective case.
Me, you, him, her, it, us, you, them
Me, you, him, her, it, us, you, them.
Object pronouns are in the objective case.
Me, you, him, her, it, us, you, them
Me, you, him, her, it, us, you, them
Me, you, him, her, it, us, you, them.

Sentences to Analyze

Before you begin, make sure that you mark the conjunctions with wings. The questions that have been added to your analysis script are there to help you analyze the sentence.

S PV
Tom took one (apple) and (some cake)
adj do adj do

a. (First, read the sentence aloud.) "Tom took one apple and some cake."

b. "Are there any conjunctions?" (Choral response: "Yes, sir.") (Since *and* is a conjunction, put wings before and after it.)

c. "The order of analysis is phrases, clauses, principal elements, modifiers."

d. "Are there any prepositional phrases?" (Choral response: "No, sir." Since there are none, you can answer *no*, and continue.)

e. "This is a sentence, and it is declarative."

f. "This sentence is about *Tom*. So, *Tom* is the subject because it is what the sentence is about." (Since *Tom* is the subject, underline it and place a capital letter *S* above it.)

g. "This sentence tells us that Tom *took*. So, *took* is the predicate because it is what the sentence tells us about *Tom*." (Since *took* tells something about Tom, double underline the predicate and a capital letter *P* above it.) "It is a predicate verb because it shows action. There is no linking verb because predicate verbs do not need linking verbs." (Since *took* shows action, place a capital letter *V* to the right of the letter *P* above the predicate.)

h. "*Apple* and *cake* tell us what Tom took." (Since *apple* and *cake* tell what Tom took, draw a circle around each of them.)

i. "So, *apple* and *cake* are objective elements because they complete the meaning of an action verb. They are direct objects because they tell *what* Tom took." (Write *do* in lowercase letters beneath each direct object.)

j. “*And* is the conjunction.”

k. “*Some* tells us *how much* of the cake Tom took. So, *some* is an adjective element because it modifies a noun. It is an adjective.” (Since *some* is an adjective, draw a straight line down from the adjective, then a horizontal line toward the word that it modifies, and then a straight line with an arrow pointing to the word it modifies. Write *adj* in lowercase letters in the elbow opposite the line with the arrow.)

l. “*One* tells us *how many* apples Tom took. So *one* is an adjective element because it modifies a noun. It is an adjective.” (Since *one* is an adjective, draw a straight line down from the adjective, then a horizontal line toward the word that it modifies, and then a straight line with an arrow pointing to the word it modifies. Write *adj* in lowercase letters in the elbow opposite the line with the arrow.)

If you were really hungry when the server came to take your order at a restaurant, you would probably not waste words saying, “I would like a cheeseburger. I would like french fries. I would like applesauce.” You would more likely apply the “less is more” principle to get your order placed more quickly: “I would like a cheeseburger, french fries, and applesauce.” Now, that’s an effective use of a compound direct object. But don’t forget to add *please*!

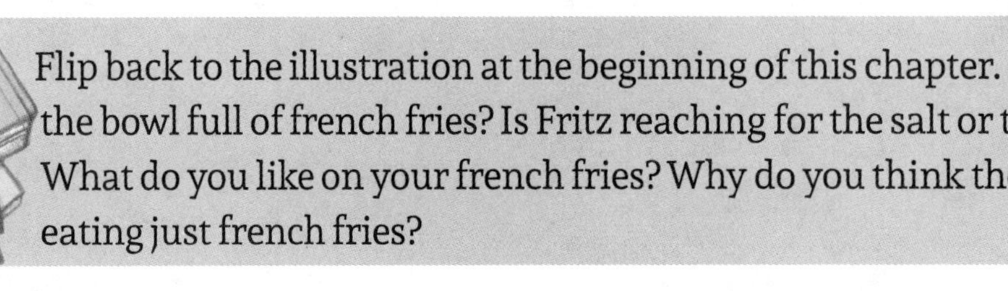

Flip back to the illustration at the beginning of this chapter. Did you notice the bowl full of french fries? Is Fritz reaching for the salt or the ketchup? What do you like on your french fries? Why do you think the family is eating just french fries?

Notes

Introductory Lesson
Compound Direct Objects

Review It

You now know that the more you recite, the more you remember. See if you can recite answers to the following questions:

What is a direct object? What are the four classes of verbs?

What is a transitive verb? What is an intransitive verb?

Learn It

A sentence is a group of words that express a complete thought. The order of the words is important for the sentence to make sense. Construct sentences using the following strings of words.

Example: afternoon, somersaults, Heidi, during, did, long, the
During the long afternoon, Heidi did somersaults.

1. bone, table, Rex, steak, gobbled, under, the, the.

____

____

2. shovel, neighbor, back, little, brought, yesterday, the, the.

____

____

3. break, Dad, garage, spring, whole, organized, after, the, the

____

____

4. clay, potter, carefully, gray, old, shaped, the, the

____

____

Analyze It

Analyze the following sentences (*S* = subject; *PV* = predicate verb; *hv* = helping verb; *adv* = adverb; *adj* = adjective; *do* = direct object; *p* = preposition; *op* = object of the preposition; *prep* = prepositional phrase).

1. During the storm, the rain watered the flowers and plants.

2. Unfortunately the tree branch hit the window and wooden bench.

Introductory Practice
Compound Direct Objects

1. Analyze the following sentences (*S* = subject; *PV* = predicate verb; *hv* = helping verb; *adv* = adverb; *adj* = adjective; *do* = direct object; *p* = preposition; *op* = object of the preposition; *prep* = prepositional phrase).

   a. At the restaurant, the waitress gave crayons and doodle sheets to the kids.

   b. The three children nibbled saltines and breadsticks at the table.

   c. Dad told riddles and jokes during the long wait.

   d. Finally she brought the hamburgers and french fries to them.

2. On the lines provided, list the *compound direct objects* adverbs from the above sentences.

   a. ______________________ b. ______________________

   c. ______________________ d. ______________________

   e. ______________________ f. ______________________

   g. ______________________ h. ______________________

3. Construct a sentence using the following string of words: *sky, soars, bird, blue, the, the, in.*

___

___

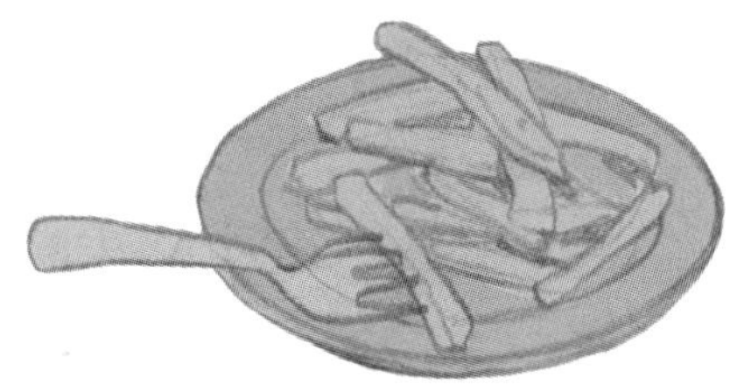

Lessons to Learn
Compound Direct Objects

Review It

Give complete answers to the following statements and questions.

List the four classes of verbs.

What are the four classes of verbs?

Construct a sentence with a transitive verb.

What is a direct object?

Construct a sentence with a compound direct object.

What is the direct object in the sentence that you constructed?

To the Source:

■ **proper & common**

The Latin word for *common* is *communis*, meaning "public, shared by many, or general." The Latin word for *proper* is *proprius*, meaning "one's own, particular to itself."

Learn It

The two classes of nouns are proper■ and common■ nouns. Remember, a proper noun names a particular person, place, or thing and is always capitalized. Common nouns are all other nouns and may be preceded by an article adjective. Identify the class of nouns to which each of the following words belongs and, on the lines provided, write a complete sentence that tells how you know each noun is common or proper.

Example:

bulbs: **It is common because it names any bulbs.**
Aunt Gabby: **It is proper because it names a particular person.**

1. jump rope ______________________________

____

2. Holland ______________________________

____

3. tulips ____

____

4. Michigan ____

____

5. brothers ____

____

6. fence ____

____

7. Fritz ____

____

Analyze It

Analyze the following sentences (*S* = subject; *PV* = predicate verb; *hv* = helping verb; *adv* = adverb; *adj* = adjective; *do* = direct object; *p* = preposition; *op* = object of the preposition; *prep* = prepositional phrase).

1. Will they be having hamburgers or cheeseburgers at the picnic?

2. Mom is bringing a pasta salad and a Caesar salad for it also.

Lessons to Practice
Compound Direct Objects

1. Analyze the following sentences (*S* = subject; *PV* = predicate verb; *hv* = helping verb; *adv* = adverb; *adj* = adjective; *do* = direct object; *p* = preposition; *op* = object of the preposition; *prep* = prepositional phrase).

   a. The two kids lifted the thick branches and green leaves.

   b. In the bushes, a secret nest had one blue egg and one white egg.

   c. Theo noticed shells and feathers on the ground.

   d. For science class, Peggy collected the eggshells and tiny feathers.

2. Identify the class of each of the following nouns by writing *proper* or *common* in the blank.

   a. Mrs. Smith ______________________________

   b. farmer ______________________________

   c. sister ______________________________

d. Theo ______________________________

e. carrot ______________________________

f. sandbox ______________________________

g. Ohio ______________________________

h. neighbor ______________________________

3. Construct a sentence using the following string of words: *deep, several, swim, sea, fish, the, in.*

____

____

Lessons to Learn
Compound Direct Objects

Review It

Think about object pronouns. Can you list all eight? See if you can create eight compound direct objects; each compound should include at least one of the object pronouns.

Example: *me*
Mom and *me*.

Learn It

Direct objects complete the meaning of the action verb. In the following sentences, fill in the missing part of the compound direct object.

Example: Dad watched Theo and ___the boys___ in his fields.

1. Theo played soccer and ______________________________ near the new playground.
2. Four little cousins played tag and ______________________________ on the blacktop.
3. During the game, the kids shared nachos and ______________________________ with the other kids.
4. Afterward, Theo put away the equipment and ______________________________ into the gray crate near the wooden shed.

B

Lessons to Learn
Compound Direct Objects

Analyze It

Analyze the following sentences (*S* = subject; *PV* = predicate verb; *hv* = helping verb; *adv* = adverb; *adj* = adjective; *do* = direct object; *p* = preposition; *op* = object of the preposition; *prep* = prepositional phrase).

1. Grandma helped the cousins and me with the project.

2. Did you gather from the floor all the felt pieces and cotton balls?

Lessons to Practice
Compound Direct Objects

B

1. Analyze the following sentences (*S* = subject; *PV* = predicate verb; *hv* = helping verb; *adv* = adverb; *adj* = adjective; *do* = direct object; *p* = preposition; *op* = object of the preposition; *prep* = prepositional phrase).

    a. During the rainy afternoon, Mom quietly read fables and fairytales to Fritz.

    b. Will Heidi now play chess or checkers with Winston?

    c. In the corner, a gray spider slowly spun sticky threads and circular webs for a trap.

    d. Stripes watched the sneaky spider and a clueless black fly.

2. Identify the class of each of the following nouns by writing *proper* or *common* in the blank.

   a. Missouri ______________________________

   b. firefighter ______________________________

   c. swing set ______________________________

   d. October ______________________________

   e. Stripes ______________________________

   f. Monday ______________________________

3. Construct a sentence using the following string of words: *enjoyment, read, books, children, for, those.*

   ____

   ____

Lessons to Learn
Compound Direct Objects

Review It

Answer the following questions:

What are two classes of nouns?

What are the four classes of verbs?

What is a direct object?

What is a compound direct object?

What are object pronouns?

Name a plural, third-person object pronoun.

Learn It

Construct sentences with compound direct objects by adding another direct object and conjunction to each of the following sentences.

Example: In the room, he opened the closet <u>and dresser drawers</u>.

1. Winston took from the shelf the tennis racket ____________________

   ____.

2. Next he swatted the pillows ____________________________________

   ____.

3. Then he hit the old socks _______________________________________

   ____.

4. Did Winston just invent pillow tennis ______________________

____?

Analyze It

Analyze the following sentences (*S* = subject; *PV* = predicate verb; *hv* = helping verb; *adv* = adverb; *adj* = adjective; *do* = direct object; *p* = preposition; *op* = object of the preposition; *prep* = prepositional phrase).

1. Under the bridge, the fishermen caught trout and walleye.

2. On the shore, the other fishermen built a fire pit and a small fire.

Lessons to Practice
Compound Direct Objects

1. Analyze the following sentences (*S* = subject; *PV* = predicate verb; *hv* = helping verb; *adv* = adverb; *adj* = adjective; *do* = direct object; *p* = preposition; *op* = object of the preposition; *prep* = prepositional phrase).

   a. On Saturday, the family carried the brownies and cookies to the school fair.

   b. Winston threw the spongy ball and the softball at the target.

   c. May I have caramel corn or an orange slushy?

   d. At the end, Mr. Wilson awarded the first-place poem and best sketch.

2. Identify the class of each of the following nouns by writing *proper* or *common* in the blank.

   a. hands ______________________________

   b. Coach Stevens ______________________________

   c. Big Dipper ______________________________

   d. daffodils ______________________________

e. wave ______________________________

f. cloud ______________________________

3. Construct a sentence using the following string of words: *work, make, hands, light, many, the.*

____

____

Review It

Answer the following questions.

What are the four classes of verbs?

What is a direct object?

What is a transitive verb?

What are object pronouns?

Name a plural, first-person object pronoun.

Name a singular, second-person object pronoun.

Learn It

Construct a sentence with a compound direct object. Choose one noun from the list below or from the class "noun jar." Add a noun of your own to form the compound direct object. Then, construct the rest of the sentence. See how many sentences you can make.

Example: ***hammer***
Uncle Ulysses uses the *hammer* and *nails*.

cups	cupcake	spade	pepper	sprinkler
blanket	ducklings	crocus	ketchup	Fritz
shoes	pickle	bread	cheese	pencils
table	skates	story	books	milk
sandwich	fork	baseball	peanuts	hands

On the lines provided, write your favorite newly constructed sentence.

____

____

Lessons to Practice—Review
Compound Direct Objects

1. Analyze the following sentences: (*S* = subject; *PV* = predicate verb; *hv* = helping verb; *adv* = adverb; *adj* = adjective; *do* = direct object; *p* = preposition; *op* = object of the preposition; *prep* = prepositional phrase).

   a. After school, the scouts followed the van and buses to the nature center.

   b. Unfortunately Theo left the water bottles and snack bags on the bus.

   c. Fourteen hungry boys rode horses and ponies through the grassy fields.

   d. The scouts later saw field hawks and black ravens in the meadow.

2. Identify the class of each of the following nouns by writing *proper* or *common* in the blank.

   a. Texas ______________________________

   b. cherries ______________________________

   c. patriot ______________________________

d. Thursday ______________________________

e. thumb ______________________________

f. Peggy ______________________________

3. Construct a sentence using the following string of words: *alone, the, the, tree, apple, boy, climbed, young.*

____

____

Notes

Lessons to Enjoy—Poem
Compound Direct Objects

Christopher Morley was an American poet who loved to write. In the poem "Animal Crackers," the narrator describes his favorite indulgence (special treat) using clever words and delicious images. Do you have a favorite after-school treat or dessert? Make a class list of favorites.

Animal Crackers

by Christopher Morley (1890–1957)

Animal crackers, and cocoa to drink,
That is the finest of suppers, I think;
When I'm grown up and can have what I please
I think I shall always insist upon these.

What do you choose when you're offered a treat?
When Mother says, "What would you like best to eat?"
Is it waffles and syrup, or cinnamon toast?
It's cocoa and animals that *I* love the most!

The kitchen's the coziest place that I know:
The kettle is singing, the stove is aglow,
And there in the twilight, how jolly to see
The cocoa and animals waiting for me.

Daddy and Mother dine later in state,
With Mary to cook for them, Susan to wait,
But they don't have nearly as much fun as I
Who eat in the kitchen with Nurse standing by;
And Daddy once said, he would like to be me
Having cocoa and animals once more for tea![1]

in state: formally

nurse: a nanny or woman who is hired to help take care of little children

1. Christopher Morley, "Animal Crackers," in *Favorite Poems Old and New*, ed. Helen Ferris (New York: Doubleday & Company, Inc., 1957), p. 43.

Questions to Ponder

1. What is the speaker's favorite supper?
2. What is the coziest place for the speaker to enjoy a treat? Why?
3. What does "the kettle is singing, the stove is aglow" mean?
4. Is the person speaking in the poem a grown man or a child?

The Curious Child's Literary Appendix

In each chapter, we have used a classic poem or excerpt from a classic book to illustrate the grammatical principles taught in that chapter. Reading just a few lines from a fine piece of literature is like getting a small sample of something savory (delicious) at the grocery store. That is called "whetting your appetite." If you want more, you beg to be allowed to buy what you only tasted.

Have you been tantalized by any of the literary samples? If so, you can find the fuller feast here in this appendix. All the poems are presented in their entirety. All the excerpts from fiction are presented in more detail to whet (sharpen) your appetite for the whole book from which they are taken.

Of course, you can really treat yourself to a banquet at the library, where you can check out and read the novels or entire collections of poetry. *Bon appetit!* (Enjoy!)

Chapter 1

Charlotte's Web

From chapter 6, "Summer Days"

by E.B. White (1899–1985)

"Look," he began in his sharp voice, "you say you have seven goslings. There were eight eggs. What happened to the other egg? Why didn't it hatch?"

goslings: baby geese

"It's a dud, I guess," said the goose.

"What are you going to do with it?" continued Templeton, his little round beady eyes fixed on the goose.

beady: small, round, and shiny
fixed: stared

"You can have it," replied the goose. "Roll it away and add it to that nasty collection of yours." (Templeton had a habit of picking up unusual objects around the farm and storing them in his home. He saved everything.)

"Certainly-ertainly-ertainly," said the gander. "You may have the egg. But I'll tell you one thing, Templeton, if I ever catch you poking-oking-oking your ugly nose around our goslings, I'll give you the worst pounding a rat ever took." And the gander opened his strong wings and beat the air with them to show his power. He was strong and brave, but the truth is, both the goose and the gander were worried about Templeton. And with good reason. The rat had no morals, no conscience, no scruples, no consideration, no decency, no milk of rodent kindness, no compunctions, no higher feeling, no friendliness, no anything. He would kill a gosling if he could get away with it—the goose knew that.

gander: male goose

pounding: beating

morals: standards or acceptable ways to behave or believe
conscience: an inner, guiding feeling about right or wrong
scruples: restraint from doing wrong

Everybody knew it.[1]

consideration: careful thought over a period of time
decency: behavior that is acceptable and proper
milk of rodent kindness: compassion or goodness (a play on the phrase "milk of human kindness")
compunctions: uneasiness about the rightness of an action
higher feeling: sentiment or warm wishes

1. E.B. White, "Summer Days," *Charlotte's Web* (New York: HarperTrophy, 1980), pp. 45–46.

Chapter 2

Just So Stories

From chapter 7, "The Beginning of the Armadillos"

by Rudyard Kipling (1865–1936)

'But I *am* Tortoise,' said Slow-and-Solid. 'Your mother was quite right. She said that you were to scoop me out of my shell with your paw. Begin.'

'You didn't say she said that a minute ago,' said Painted Jaguar, sucking the prickles out of his paddy-paw. 'You said she said something quite different.'

prickles: small, sharp points like thorns

'Well, suppose you say that I said that she said something quite different, I don't see that it makes any difference; because if she said what you said I said she said, it's just the same as if I said what she said she said. On the other hand, if you think she said that you were to uncoil me with a scoop, instead of pawing me into drops with a shell, I can't help that, can I?'

'But you said you wanted to be scooped out of your shell with my paw,' said Painted Jaguar.

'If you'll think again you'll find that I didn't say anything of the kind. I said that your mother said that you were to scoop me out of my shell,' said Slow-and-Solid.

'What will happen if I do?' said the Jaguar most sniffily and most cautious.

sniffily: showing contempt (lack of respect) or haughtiness (pridefulness)

'I don't know, because I've never been scooped out of my shell before; but I tell you truly, if you want to see me swim away you've only got to drop me into the water.'

'I don't believe it,' said Painted Jaguar.[1]

1. Rudyard Kipling, "The Beginning of the Armadillos," *Just So Stories* (New York: Doubleday, 1952), p. 39.

Chapter 3

Moon Folly

by Fannie Stearns Davis (1884–1966)

I will go up the mountain after the Moon:
She is caught in a dead fir-tree.
Like a great pale apple of silver and pearl,
Like a great pale apple is she.

I will leap and will clasp her with quick cold hands
And carry her home in my sack.
I will set her down safe on the oaken bench
That stands at the chimney-back.

And then I will sit by the fire all night,
And sit by the fire all day.
I will gnaw at the Moon to my heart's delight,
Till I gnaw her slowly away.

And while I grow mad with the Moon's cold taste,
The World may beat on my door,
Crying "Come out!" and crying "Make haste!
And give us the Moon once more!"

But I shall not answer them ever at all;
I will laugh, as I count and hide
The great black beautiful seeds of the Moon
In a flower-pot deep and wide.

Then I will lie down and go fast asleep,
Drunken with flame and aswoon.
But the seeds will sprout, and the seeds will leap:
The subtle swift seeds of the Moon.

aswoon: dazed or light headed

subtle: delicate or obscure

And some day, all of the world that beats
And cries at my door, shall see
A thousand moon-leaves spring from my thatch
On a marvelous white Moon-tree!

Then each shall have Moons to his heart's desire:
Apples of silver and pearl:
Apples of orange and copper fire,
Setting his five wits aswirl.

aswirl: swirling

And then they will thank me, who mock me now,
"Wanting the Moon is he!"
Oh, I'm off to the mountain after the Moon,
Ere she falls from the dead fir-tree![1]

1. Fannie Stearns Davis, "Moon Folly" from In Poetry, Vol. I, ed. Harriet Monroe (New York: A.M.S. Reprint CO, Vol. 1, No. 6, March 1912–1913), pp. 183–184. Available at: https://books.google.com/books?id=9MARAAAAYAAJ.

Chapter 4

The Wind in the Willows

From chapter 3, "The Wild Wood"

by Kenneth Grahame (1859–1932)

In the winter time the Rat slept a great deal, retiring early and rising late. During his short day he sometimes scribbled poetry or did other small domestic jobs about the house; and, of course, there were always animals dropping in for a chat, and consequently there was a good deal of story-telling and comparing notes on the past summer and all its doings.

domestic: household

Such a rich chapter it had been, when one came to look back on it all! With illustrations so numerous and so very highly coloured! The pageant of the river bank had marched steadily along, unfolding itself in scene-pictures that succeeded each other in stately procession. Purple loosestrife arrived early, shaking luxuriant tangled locks along the edge of the mirror whence its own face laughed back at it. Willow-herb, tender and wistful, like a pink sunset cloud, was not slow to follow. Comfrey, the purple hand-in-hand with the white, crept forth to take its place in the line; and at last one morning the diffident and delaying dog-rose stepped delicately on the stage, and one knew, as if string-music had announced it in stately chords that strayed into a gavotte, that June at last was here.[1]

coloured: colored
pageant: a parade or procession
stately: grand manner; dignified
loosestrife: a purple wildflower
luxuriant: lush
whence: from which
willow-herb: a wildflower
wistful: quiet, silent, regretful
comfrey: wildflower
diffident: bashful
dog-rose: a pink or white wildflower
gavotte: a French dance

1. Kenneth Grahame, "The Wild Wood," *The Wind in the Willows* (New York: The New American Library, Inc., 1969), pp. 56–57.

Chapter 5

The Walrus and the Carpenter

by Lewis Carroll (1832–1898)

The sun was shining on the sea,
   Shining with all his might:
He did his very best to make
   The billows smooth and bright—
And this was odd, because it was
   The middle of the night.

billows: waves

The moon was shining sulkily,
   Because she thought the sun
Had got no business to be there
   After the day was done—
'It's very rude of him,' she said,
   'To come and spoil the fun.'

sulkily: unhappily

The sea was wet as wet could be,
   The sands were dry as dry.
You could not see a cloud, because
   No cloud was in the sky:
No birds were flying overhead—
   There were no birds to fly.

The Walrus and the Carpenter
   Were walking close at hand:
They wept like anything to see
   Such quantities of sand:
'If this were only cleared away,'
   They said, 'it would be grand!'

'If seven maids with seven mops
   Swept it for half a year,
Do you suppose,' the Walrus said,
   'That they could get it clear?'

'I doubt it,' said the Carpenter,
And shed a bitter tear.

'O Oysters, come and walk with us!'
The Walrus did beseech.
'A pleasant walk, a pleasant talk,
Along the briny beach:
We cannot do with more than four,
To give a hand to each.'

beseech: beg

briny: salty water

The eldest Oyster looked at him,
But never a word he said:
The eldest Oyster winked his eye,
And shook his heavy head—
Meaning to say he did not choose
To leave the oyster-bed.

But four young Oysters hurried up,
All eager for the treat:
Their coats were brushed, their faces washed,
Their shoes were clean and neat—
And this was odd, because, you know,
They hadn't any feet.

Four other Oysters followed them,
And yet another four;
And thick and fast they came at last,
And more, and more, and more—
All hopping through the frothy waves,
And scrambling to the shore.

frothy: foamy, bubbly
scrambling: struggle clumsily

The Walrus and the Carpenter
Walked on a mile or so,
And then they rested on a rock
Conveniently low:
And all the little Oysters stood
And waited in a row.

'The time has come,' the Walrus said,
'To talk of many things:

Of shoes—and ships—and sealing wax—
   Of cabbages—and kings—
And why the sea is boiling hot—
   And whether pigs have wings.'

'But wait a bit,' the Oysters cried,
   'Before we have our chat;
For some of us are out of breath,
   And all of us are fat!'
'No hurry!' said the Carpenter.
   They thanked him much for that.

'A loaf of bread,' the Walrus said,
   'Is what we chiefly need:
Pepper and vinegar besides
   Are very good indeed—
Now if you're ready, Oysters dear,
   We can begin to feed.'

'But not on us!' the Oysters cried,
   Turning a little blue.
'After such kindness, that would be
   A dismal thing to do!'
'The night is fine,' the Walrus said.
   'Do you admire the view?'

dismal: terrible, dark

'It was so kind of you to come!
   And you are very nice!'
The Carpenter said nothing but
   'Cut us another slice--
I wish you were not quite so deaf—
   I've had to ask you twice!'

'It seems a shame,' the Walrus said,
   'To play them such a trick,
After we've brought them out so far,
   And made them trot so quick!'
The Carpenter said nothing but
   'The butter's spread too thick!'

trot: run at a slow, steady pace

'I weep for you,' the Walrus said:
  'I deeply sympathize.'
With sobs and tears he sorted out
  Those of the largest size,
Holding his pocket-handkerchief
  Before his streaming eyes.

sympathize: express pity or compassion

'O Oysters,' said the Carpenter,
  'You've had a pleasant run!
Shall we be trotting home again?'
  But answer came there none—
And this was scarcely odd, because
  They'd eaten every one.[1]

1. Lewis Carroll, "The Walrus and the Carpenter," *Through the Looking-Glass* (New York: Random House, 1916), pp. 56–61.

Chapter 6

Just So Stories

From "How the Whale Got His Throat"

by Rudyard Kipling (1865–1936)

'Noble and generous Cetacean, have you ever tasted Man?'

'No,' said the Whale. 'What is it like?'

'Nice,' said the small 'Stute Fish. 'Nice but nubbly.'

'Then fetch me some,' said the Whale, and he made the sea froth up with his tail.

'One at a time is enough,' said the 'Stute Fish. 'If you swim to latitude Fifty North, longitude Forty West (that is magic), you will find, sitting *on* a raft, *in* the middle of the sea, with nothing on but a pair of blue canvas breeches, a pair of suspenders (you must *not* forget the suspenders, Best Beloved), and a jack-knife, one shipwrecked Mariner, who, it is only fair to tell you, is a man of infinite-resource-and-sagacity.'

So the Whale swam and swam to latitude Fifty North, longitude Forty West, as fast as he could swim, and *on* a raft *in* the middle of the sea, *with* nothing to wear except a pair of blue canvas breeches, a pair of suspenders (you must particularly remember the suspenders, Best Beloved), *and* a jack-knife, he found one single, solitary shipwrecked Mariner, trailing his toes in the water. (He had his mummy's leave to paddle, or else he would never have done it, because he was a man of infinite-resource-and-sagacity.)

Then the Whale opened his mouth back and back and back till it nearly touched his tail, and he swallowed the shipwrecked Mariner, and the raft he was sitting on, and his blue canvas breeches, and the suspenders (which you *must*

Cetacean: whale

nubbly: rough or irregular, textured

froth: small bubbles, foam

latitude: the distance north or south of the equator measured in degrees
longitude: distance measured by degrees or time east or west between the North and South Poles
breeches: short pants that are fastened just below the knee
suspenders: a pair of straps that pass over the shoulders and fasten to the waist of pants or a skirt
Mariner: sailor
infinite: unlimited, never ending
sagacity: quality of being wise or having good judgment

not forget), *and* the jack-knife—He swallowed them all down into his warm, dark, inside cupboards, and then he smacked his lips—so, and turned round three times on his tail.[1]

1. Rudyard Kipling, "How the Whale Got His Throat," *Just So Stories* (New York: Doubleday, CO, 1952), p. 9.

Chapter 7

"A Good Play"

by Robert Louis Stevenson (1850–1894)

We built a ship upon the stairs,
All made of back-bedroom chairs,
And filled it full of sofa pillows
To go a-sailing on the billows.

billows: a great swell or surge of water

We took a saw and several nails,
And water in the nursery pails;
And Tom said, "Let us also take
An apple and a slice of cake";—
Which was enough for Tom and me
To go a-sailing on, till tea.

tea: for the British, any meal eaten in the late afternoon or early evening

We sailed along for days and days,
And had the very best of plays;
But Tom fell out and hurt his knee,
So there was no one left but me.[1]

1. Robert Louis Stevenson, "A Good Play," in *Favorite Poems Old and New*, ed. Helen Ferris (New York: Doubleday & Company, Inc., 1957), pp. 101–102.

Biographies
Meet the Authors

Aesop *(c. 620–564 BC)*[1]

Everything we know about the ancient Greek fable teller Aesop is speculation. His life story itself may be a fable. That makes Aesop legendary. According to tradition, he lived in the sixth century BC and told his animal stories orally. The story goes that Aesop was a slave who was extremely ugly, even misshapen, but he was also extraordinarily clever. He was able to win his freedom through his wit, revealing to his master surprising truths beneath the surface of everyday life. In the end, he became an advisor to kings. Aesop's fables were passed down through generations of storytellers until finally, about 300 years after he told them, the fables were written down in a collection. The fables, such as "The Tortoise and the Hare," feature tales of animals who behave like humans and demonstrate moral lessons through their folly. (See chapters 1, 2, 3, and 6.)

Carroll, Lewis *(1832–1898)*[2]

Charles Lutwidge Dodgson, born in England in 1832, was a successful mathematician, university professor, and deacon who used the pen name Lewis Carroll when he published nonsense literature, a kind of writing that combines things that make sense with things that do not. Carroll's poems "The Walrus and the Carpenter" and "Jabberwocky" are considered superb examples of literary nonsense. While on a picnic one day in 1862, he made up a complex nonsensical tale to entertain his young friend, Alice Liddel, and her sisters. The result is his world famous *Alice's Adventures in Wonderland*. Carroll stammered when he talked and, playing with the sound of his last name, Dodgson, referred to himself as the Dodo, who appears in the book. Carroll died of pneumonia in 1898, better known for his children's books than for his mathematics. (See chapter 5 and the literary appendix.)

Davis, Fannie Stearns *(1884–1966)*[3]

Fannie Stearns Davis was an English teacher and poet who graduated from Smith College in 1904 during a time when many women did not have access to college educations. Editor of the classic history book, *A Day in Old Athens*, which was authored by her well-known brother William, Fannie Stearns Davis should not be forgotten for her own writing. She published two volumes of poetry, *Myself and I* in 1913 and *Crack O' Dawn* in 1915, which have appealed to many modern readers. For example, folk singer Jan Luby recently set Davis's poem "Moon Folly" to music. Davis was born in Cleveland, Ohio, in 1884 and died in 1966. (See chapter 3 and the literary appendix.)

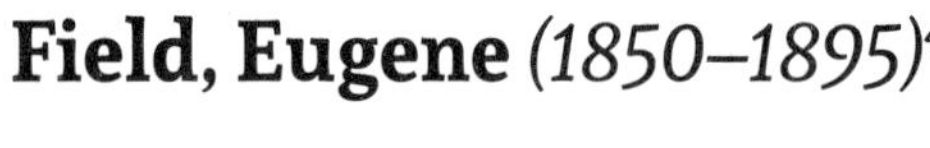

Field, Eugene *(1850–1895)*[4]

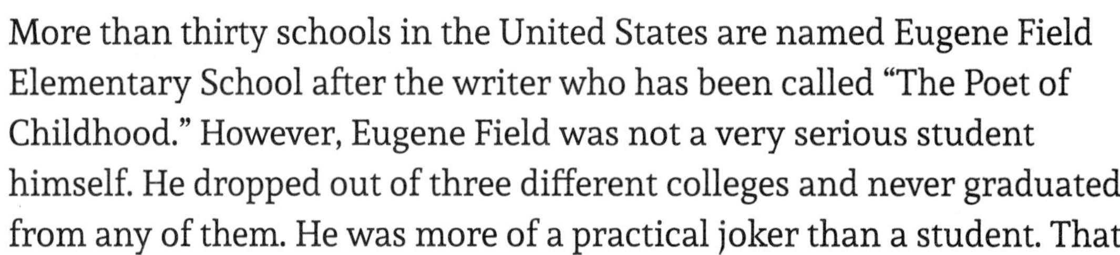

More than thirty schools in the United States are named Eugene Field Elementary School after the writer who has been called "The Poet of Childhood." However, Eugene Field was not a very serious student himself. He dropped out of three different colleges and never graduated from any of them. He was more of a practical joker than a student. That sense of humor served him well as he made a living from writing satirical columns for newspapers to support his wife and eight children. Field may have been a journalist in the adult world, but for children he wrote poem after charming poem, including "The Gingham Dog and the Calico Cat" and "The Sugar-Plum Tree." He was often caught making funny faces at children in public when he thought no one else was watching. Field advised reading in bed because, as he wrote, "no book can be appreciated until it has been slept with and dreamed over."[5] He was born in St. Louis, Missouri, in 1850 and died in 1895 at the age of forty-five in Chicago. (See chapter 5.)

Grahame, Kenneth *(1859–1932)*[6]

When Kenneth Grahame was little, he lived near the River Thames in England, where he learned how to row a boat. Exploring the river and the nearby woods inspired him years later to tell his son Alistair stories about the animals encountered there. In his stories the animals act and dress like humans, and one of them—Toad—is as strong-willed as it is said Alistair himself was. Later, the tales would become Grahame's most enduring book, *The Wind in the Willows*. Grahame was born in Scotland in 1859 and did not even start going to school until he was nine years old. By the time he graduated, though, he had won a number of academic and athletic awards. Unable to afford to go to Oxford University as he wished, he worked as a banker for years, all along continuing to write stories and essays. By the time of his death in 1932, Grahame was an acclaimed author. (See chapter 4 and the literary appendix.)

Kipling, Rudyard *(1865–1936)*[7]

Even though he spent most of his life in England and America, Rudyard Kipling always considered his home to be India, where he was born in 1865. As a youth, he explored the busy markets of Bombay, learned the native language, and came to appreciate the people and culture of India. One collection of his stories for children, *The Jungle Book*, is set in India and includes stories about a boy named Mowgli who is raised by wolves. Like many children's authors, Kipling first told his stories aloud to his own family. His daughter Josephine used to ask him to tell his tales "just so" or exactly as he told them before. That's how his series of *Just So Stories* got its title. Kipling published many poems, stories, essays, and books for adults too. He was awarded the Nobel Prize in Literature in 1907 partly because he was so accomplished in narration. He died in 1936 in London. (See chapters 2 and 6 and the literary appendix.)

Lear, Edward *(1812–1888)*[8]

Edward Lear, who had twenty siblings, was raised by his oldest sister after his impoverished family had to split up. He became a serious artist, traveling widely from his English birthplace. He illustrated books about plants and animals, and he painted landscapes of the places he visited. Remembered today mostly for writing nonsense, as in his collection of poetry called *The Book of Nonsense*, Lear often created silly animal characters and illustrated his poems with his own pen-and-ink drawings. Wanderers like Lear himself, his characters are often on journeys, such as "The Owl and the Pussycat" going "off to sea in a beautiful pea green boat."[9] Lear had a special talent for writing limericks (a humorous form of poetry he made popular) and for making up neologisms (new words that sound real but are actually nonsense), such as the owl and pussy-cat's *runcible* spoon. Although he had many close friends, he died alone in 1888 at his villa on the Mediterranean coast. (See chapter 2.)

Morley, Christopher *(1890–1957)*[10]

An American "man of letters" (a person dedicated to reading and writing), Christopher Morley was a poet, novelist, essayist, playwright, journalist, and editor. He was immersed in the world of writers and publishers for his entire career, and he was admired both for his wit and his kindness. He was born in Pennsylvania in 1890 to English parents who valued education highly. His father was a professor; his musician mother taught him to love literature; two of his brothers, like himself, were awarded prestigious Rhodes Scholarships, which allowed them to study at Oxford University in England. Morley's favorite place to write was in a cabin he called the Knothole. He built it himself on the property where he lived with his wife and four children. In 1951, he suffered a series of strokes which kept him from writing as much as he wanted in the last years of his life. He died in 1957. (See chapter 7.)

Morris, George Pope *(1802–1864)*[11]

Born in Philadelphia in 1802, George Pope Morris was a successful and respected journalist and editor in New York in the early nineteenth century. He founded several magazines, one of which is still published under the title *Town & Country*, but he was most revered as a poet and songwriter. His work was so popular even after his death in 1864 that Union soldiers sang his patriotic lyrics during the Civil War in their encampments. "Woodman, Spare That Tree," perhaps his most famous poem-song, is sometimes quoted or its title paraphrased by environmentalists today. It was set to music shortly after it was first published. Back then, CDs and electronic devices didn't exist, so instead people bought sheet music so they could play a song at home on an instrument and sing along. Morris published many such poems as songs with beautifully illustrated title pages. (See chapter 1.)

Rossetti, Christina *(1830–1894)*[12]

Considered one of the most important English poets of her time, Christina Rossetti wrote in a broad range of styles and about many different topics: both children's and adult literature; both fantastic and religious works; both lighthearted, humorous poems and dark, brooding ones. Born in 1830, she grew into a beautiful young woman and was a model for her brother, Dante Gabriel Rossetti, who was a famous painter, poet, illustrator, and translator. She was high spirited and passionate and worked hard her whole life to control her temper. Relying on a deep faith in God, she considered spiritual beauty, rather than physical beauty, most important, so she devoted herself to writing and to the people she loved. She died in London in 1894. In the midst of all her accomplishments, one of her children's books stands out as particularly musical and witty. *Sing-Song: A Nursery Rhyme Book* includes some poems that teach children virtues such as patience, some that help children remember a lesson such as the order of the months, and some with playful rhymes and rhythms that are just plain fun for children. (See chapter 6.)

Shakespeare, William *(1564–1616)*

Perhaps the most esteemed English writer of all time, William Shakespeare is a bit of a mystery. We don't know much for sure about his life, except for bits of information found in public records. He was born on April 23, 1564—we think—and he died on his birthday in 1616. He was raised in Stratford-upon-Avon, and that is where his wife and children lived when he was writing, performing, and producing plays in London. He was acclaimed during his own lifetime for his comedies, such as *A Midsummer Night's Dream*, and for his tragedies, such as *Romeo and Juliet*. In all, he wrote more than thirty-five plays, which, more than those of any other single playwright, have been produced throughout the years in many languages around the world. From his plays, we feel we do know a lot about Shakespeare: his love of a good story, his profound spirituality, his deep understanding of human emotions, and his clear awareness of the way people behave—sometimes foolishly, sometimes tragically, sometimes heroically. (See chapter 4.)

Stevenson, Robert Lewis *(1850–1894)*[13]

Best known for his adventure books *Treasure Island* and *Kidnapped* and for his horror story *The Strange Case of Dr. Jekyll and Mr. Hyde*, Robert Lewis Stevenson also wrote poetry, essays, short stories, other novels, and travelogues (a written work about someone's experiences while traveling). He was born in Scotland in 1850, and was often so sick as a child that he couldn't go to school regularly. He was a voracious reader and started writing stories when he was very young. At various times during his life, he wrote as he recuperated from serious illness. Even so, Stevenson traveled much in Europe and across the United States. He was quite tall and thin, and he liked to dress outlandishly and wear his hair long. One of his favorite themes to write about was the difference between being truly good and only appearing good. He died in 1894. (See chapter 7 and the literary appendix.)

White, E.B. *(1899–1985)*[14]

Named Elwyn Brooks White when he was born in New York in 1899, the author of *Charlotte's Web* never liked that name. When he grew up, he used his initials for his published writing and he let his friends call him Andy. He wrote many essays, poems, and books for adults, but perhaps his best-loved works are for children. He loved animals. The idea for *Charlotte's Web* came to him one day when he was watching a spider spin an egg sac. He also wrote *Stuart Little* about a little mouse who gets adopted by a human family, not as a pet but as a son, and *The Trumpet of the Swan* about a trumpeter swan born without a voice. White has influenced many other writers, especially with a famous book called *The Elements of Style*. Even as a successful and influential writer, he always said that writing is difficult. He died at his farm in 1985 when he was eighty-six years old. (See chapter 1 and the literary appendix.) (Image courtesy of White Literary LLC, CC BY-SA 3.0, https://commons.wikimedia.org/w/index.php?curid=14518529.)

Wylie, Elinor *(1885–1928)*[15]

No one could call Elinor Wylie a dabbler. She worked very hard as a writer, publishing four volumes of poetry and four novels in just seven years during the 1920s. Born in New Jersey in 1885 and raised in Pennsylvania, Wylie grew up privileged as part of a socially prominent family: Her grandfather had been the governor of Pennsylvania; her father served as solicitor general of the United States; her aunt was a published poet. Wylie was considered to be very beautiful, elegant, and witty. Independent and strong-willed, she made some personal decisions that brought many difficulties in her life. Through those trials, she immersed herself in books and in writing. Wylie died suddenly in 1928 from a stroke when she was only forty-three. (See chapter 3.)

Works Referenced

1. *Encyclopedia Britannica*, s.v. "Aesop: Legendary Greek Fabulist," accessed October 14, 2015, http://www.britannica.com/biography/Aesop.
   Encyclopedia of World Biography, vol. 24, s.v. "Aesop."
2. "Lewis Carroll in the Museum," *LearningMore*, Oxford University Museum of Natural History, March 29, 2006, accessed October 14, 2015, http://www.oum.ox.ac.uk/learning/pdfs/dodgson.pdf.
   Encyclopedia of World Biography, vol. 24, s.v. "Lewis Carroll."
3. *PoemHunter.com*, s.v. "Fannie Stearns Davis," accessed October 14, 2015, http://www.poemhunter.com/fannie-stearns-davis/biography/.
4. *The Poetry Foundation*, s.v. "Eugene Field," accessed October 14, 2015, http://www.poetryfoundation.org/bio/eugene-field.
5. Eugene Field, "The Luxury of Reading in Bed," *Love Affairs of a Bibliomaniac* (Whitefish, MT: Kessinger Publishing, 2005), p. 31.
   Dictionary of American Biography, s.v. "Eugene Field" (New York: Charles Scribner's Sons, 1936).
6. "Biography," *Kenneth Graham Society*, accessed October 14, 2015, http://www.kennethgrahamesociety.net/biography.htm.
   Encyclopedia of World Biography, vol. 28, s.v. "Kenneth Grahame."
7. *Biography.com*, s.v. "Rudyard Kipling," accessed October 14, 2015, http://www.biography.com/people/rudyard-kipling-9365581.
   Encyclopedia Britannica, s.v. "Rudyard Kipling," accessed October 14, 2015, http://www.britannica.com/biography/Rudyard-Kipling.
   Encyclopedia of World Biography, s.v. "Joseph Rudyard Kipling."
8. Edward Lear, *The Owl and the Pussycat*, illustrated by Jan Brett (New York: Putnam, 1991), n.p.
   Authors and Artists for Young Adults, vol. 48, s.v. "Edward Lear," *Biography in Context*. Detroit: Gale, 2003.
   The Poetry Foundation, s.v. "Edward Lear, 1812–1888," accessed October 14, 2015, http://www.poetryfoundation.org/bio/edward-lear.
9. Lear, Edward. *The Owl and the Pussycat*. Illustrated by Jan Brett. New York: Putnam, 1991.
10. C.D. Merriman, "Christopher Morley," *The Literature Network*, accessed October 14, 2105, http://www.online-literature.com/morley.
11. *Dictionary of American Biography*, s.v. "George Pope Morris" (New York: Charles Scribner's Sons, 1936).
12. *Encyclopedia Britannica*, s.v. "Christina Rossetti," accessed October 14, 2015, http://www.britannica.com/biography/Christina-Rossetti.
    Major Authors and Illustrators for Children and Young Adults, s.v. "Christina (Georgina) Rossetti" (Detroit: Gale, 2002).
13. *Encyclopedia Britannica*, s.v. "Robert Louis Stevenson," accessed October 14, 2015, http://www.britannica.com/biography/Robert-Louis-Stevenson.
    Encyclopedia of World Biography, vol. 28, s.v. "Robert Louis Stevenson."
14. *Biography.com*, s.v. "E.B. White," accessed October 14, 2015, http://www.biography.com/people/eb-white-9529308.
    Encyclopedia of World Biography, vol. 28, s.v. "E. B. White."
15. *Dictionary of American Biography*, s.v. "Elinor Morton Hoyt Wylie" (New York: Charles Scribner's Sons, 1936).
    Encyclopedia Britannica, s.v. "Elinor Wylie," accessed October 14, 2015, http://www.britannica.com/biography/Elinor-Wylie.

Bibliography
Seek the Sources

Aesop. "The Ant and the Grasshopper." In *Writing & Rhetoric Book 1: Fable.* Written by Paul Kortepeter. Camp Hill, PA: Classical Academic Press, 2013.

———. "The Dog and Her Reflection." In *Writing & Rhetoric Book 1: Fable.* Written by Paul Kortepeter. Camp Hill, PA: Classical Academic Press, 2013.

———. "The Mice in Council." In *Writing & Rhetoric Book 1: Fable.* Written by Paul Kortepeter. Camp Hill, PA: Classical Academic Press, 2013.

———. "The Shepherd Boy and the Wolf." In *Writing and Rhetoric Book 1: Fable.* Written by Paul Kortepeter. Camp Hill, PA: Classical Academic Press, 2013.

Anonymous. "The Tale of the Chinese Farmer." In *Writing & Rhetoric Book 1: Fable.* Written by Paul Kortepeter. Camp Hill, PA: Classical Academic Press, 2013.

Anonymous. "The Trees Choose a King." In *Writing & Rhetoric Book 1: Fable.* Written by Paul Kortepeter. Camp Hill, PA: Classical Academic Press, 2013.

Carroll, Lewis. "The Walrus and the Carpenter." *Through the Looking-Glass.* New York: Random House, 1916.

Davis, Fannie Stearns. "Moon Folly." From *In Poetry*, vol. I. Edited by Harriet Monroe. New York: A.M.S. Reprint CO, vol. 1, no. 6, March 1912–1913. Available at: https://books.google.com/books?id=9MARAAAAYAAJ.

Field, Eugene. "Wynken, Blynken, and Nod." In *Favorite Poems Old and New.* Edited by Helen Ferris. New York: Doubleday, 1957.

Grahame, Kenneth. "The Wild Wood." *The Wind in the Willows.* New York: The New American Library, Inc., 1969.

Kipling, Rudyard. "How the Whale Got His Throat." *Just So Stories.* New York: Doubleday, 1952.

———. "The Beginning of the Armadillos." *Just So Stories.* New York: Doubleday, 1952.

La Fontaine, Jean de. "The Hare and the Partridge." In *Writing & Rhetoric Book 1: Fable.* Written by Paul Kortepeter. Camp Hill, PA: Classical Academic Press, 2013.

Lear, Edward. "Calico Pie." *The Golden Treasury of Poetry.* Edited by Louis Untermeyer. New York: Golden Books Publishing, 1998.

Morley, Christopher. "Animal Crackers." In *Favorite Poems Old and New*. Edited by Helen Ferris. New York: Doubleday, 1957.

Morris, George Pope. "Woodman, Spare That Tree." *Favorite Poems Old and New*. Edited by Helen Ferris. New York: Doubleday, 1957.

Rossetti, Christina. "I Dug and Dug Amongst the Snow." In *Illustrated Poems and Songs for Young People*. Edited by Mrs. Lucy Sale Barker. London: George Routledge and Sons, 1885. Available at: https://books.google.com/books?id=c4ubK21PVw4C.

Shakespeare, William. "A Wood near Athens." Act II , Scene 1. *A Midsummer Night's Dream*. In *World Scope Family Library: Works of William Shakespeare*. Edited by W.G. Clark and W.A. Wright. New York: The Universal Guide, Inc., 1950.

Stevenson, Robert Louis. "A Good Play." In *Favorite Poems Old and New*. Edited by Helen Ferris. New York: Doubleday, 1957.

White, E.B. "Summer Days." *Charlotte's Web*. New York: HarperTrophy, 1980.

Wylie, Elinor. "Velvet Shoes." In *Favorite Poems Old and New*. Edited by Helen Ferris. New York: Doubleday, 1957.

Glossary of Terms

	Book & Level	Chapter
A		
Adjective: An adjective is a part of speech. It is used to describe or define the meaning of a noun or pronoun (*see also* noun, pronoun). It answers the questions *how many, whose, which one,* or *what kind.* It modifies a noun or pronoun.	1A	5
Adjective Element: A word (or a group of words) that modifies nouns or pronouns.	1A	5
Adjectival Prepositional Phrase: A group of words that includes a preposition followed by a noun or pronoun (*see* object of the preposition), and any words that modify the object of the preposition. The entire phrase is an adjective and modifies nouns or pronouns, answering the questions *how many, whose, which one,* or *what kind.* (This concept is covered in *WOL Level 2.*)	1B	3
Adverb: An adverb is a part of speech. It modifies a verb, an adjective, (or) adverb. It answers the questions *how, when,* or *where.* An adverb is a part of speech.	1A	4
Adverbial Element: A word (or a group of words) that modifies verbs, adjectives, and adverbs.	1A	4
Adverbial Prepositional Phrase: A group of words that includes a preposition followed by a noun or pronoun (*see* object of the preposition), and any words that modify the object of the preposition. The entire phrase is an adverb usually modifying a verb, answering the questions *when, where,* or *how.*	1B	3

	Book & Level	Chapter
Antecedent: The antecedent is a noun, clause, or phrase to which a pronoun refers. If the antecedent is singular, then the pronoun is singular too. But if the noun, clause, or phrase is plural, then the pronoun must be plural too. The antecedent determines which pronoun is used.	1A	7
Antonym: An antonyms is a word that has the opposite meaning of another word. For example, *night* and *day* are antonyms.	1B	6
Auxiliary Verb: *See* helping verb.	1A	3

C

Clause: A clause is a group of words containing a subject and a predicate.	1A	4
Common Noun: A noun that names any person, place, thing or idea. *See also* noun; proper noun.	1B	3
Compound Direct Object: Two or more direct objects that are joined with a conjunction and that together function as a single direct object for a transitive verb.	1B	7
Compound Subject: Two or more subjects that are joined with a conjunction and that together function as a single subject in the sentence.	1B	5
Compound Verb: Two or more verbs that are joined with a conjunction and that together function as a single verb for a single subject.	1B	6
Conjunction: A part of speech that joins words, phrases, or clauses. Conjunctions indicate the relationship between the elements that they join.	1A	1
Consonant: A letter of the alphabet that represents a constricted speech sound. The indefinite article "a" is used before words beginning with consonants (*b*, *c*, *d*, *f*, *g*, *h*, *j*, *k*, *l*, *m*, *n*, *p*, *q*, *r*, *s*, *t*, *v*, *w*, *x*, *y*, and z).	1A	5

	Book & Level	Chapter
Contraction: A shortened form of two words that uses an apostrophe in place of the letters and spaces left out. *WOL Level 1* focuses on contractions with subject pronouns and verbs, such as *I'm* for *I am* or *they've* for *they have*, and on contractions with verbs and the adverb *not*, such as *didn't* for *did not*.	1A	8

D

Declarative Sentence: One of the four kinds of sentences. It makes a statement and ends with a period.	1A	1
Definite Article: The adjective *the*. It identifies a particular noun and is placed before nouns or adjectives.	1A	5
Direct Object: A direct object is an objective element that tells what the subject is acting on. It is a noun or pronoun after a transitive verb. It answers the question *what* or *whom* after the verb and is labeled *do*.	1A	6

E

Eight Parts of Speech: The eight parts of speech are classes of words with the same kind of meaning and use. They are nouns, verbs, adjectives, adverbs, prepositions, pronouns, conjunctions, and interjections.	1A	1
Exclamatory Sentence: One of the four kinds of sentences. It expresses strong feeling and ends with an exclamation point.	1A	1

F

First Person: A grammatical category of pronouns used by the speaker to refer to himself or herself (i.e., the subject pronouns *I* or *we* and the object pronouns *me* or *us*). *See also* person.	1A	7
Fragment: A group of words that is not a complete sentence because it lacks a subject, a predicate, or both.	1B	4

	Book & Level	Chapter

G

Gender: A grammatical category or classification into which nouns and pronouns can be sorted—namely *male, female*, or *neuter*. For example: a *king* is masculine (*he* is a male); a *queen* is feminine (*she* is a female); and a *throne* is neuter (*it* is neither masculine nor feminine). *See also* neuter.	1B	2

H

Helping Verb: Helps another verb express its meaning. It is placed alongside a transitive, linking, or intransitive verb to form a verb phrase. Both words work together as one action. The helping verbs are *am, is, are, was, were, be, being, been, have, has, had, do, did, does, may, might, must, should, would, could, shall, will, can.*	1A	3
Homonym: A homonyms is a word that sounds the same but has a different meaning and sometimes spelling. For example, *bark* meaning the sound a dog makes and *bark* meaning the outer covering of a tree are homonyms.	1B	6

I

Imperative Sentence: One of the four kinds of sentences. It gives a command and ends with a period or exclamation point.	1A	1
Implied Subject: A subject that does not appear in the sentence but is indirectly expressed or suggested. *See also* subject.	1A	1
Indefinite Article: The adjective *a* or *an*. It is placed before non-specific nouns and identifies them as being singular; *a* is used before nouns or adjectives beginning with a consonant, and *an* is used before nouns or adjectives beginning with a vowel sound.	1A	5
Interjection: A part of speech that is a word or short phrase that expresses strong emotion. It is inserted into a sentence or stands alone.	1A	1
Interrogative Sentence: One of the four kinds of sentences. It asks a question and ends with a question mark.	1A	1

	Book & Level	Chapter
Intransitive Verb: A verb that does not take an objective element or join the subject to the predicate.	1A	6
Introductory Prepositional Phrase: An adverbial prepositional phrase that is located at the beginning of a sentence and modifies the verb.	1B	4

L

Linking Verb: A verb that joins the subject to the predicate. In other words, it is the glue that joins the subject either to a noun that renames the subject or to an adjective that describes the subject. Linking verbs express a state of being.	1A	3

M

Modifier: A word (or a group of words) that modifies or changes the meaning of word. Adjectives modify nouns and pronouns; adverbs usually modify verbs, but adverbs also can modify adjectives and other adverbs.	1A	4

N

Neuter: The gender of a pronoun that is neither male nor female. The pronoun *it* is neuter, and sometimes the pronouns *they* and *them* can be neuter.	1B	2
Nominative Case: The grammatical term indicating that a noun or pronoun is the subject in a sentence or a clause rather than its object. Also known as the *subjective case*.	1A	7
Noun: A noun is a part of speech. It names a person, place, or thing. A noun names a quality or an idea. A noun may be singular or plural.	1A	2
Number: A property of a noun or pronoun that tells how many. Singular in number means only one, and plural in number means more than one.	1A	3

	Book & Level	Chapter
O		
Object of the Preposition: The noun or pronoun after the preposition. It is joined by the preposition to another word in the sentence in a modifying relationship.	1B	1
Object Pronoun: A personal pronoun that is used as a direct object or the object of the preposition (i.e., *me, us, you, him, her, it, them*).	1A	7
Objective Element: A word or group of words that completes the meaning of the action verb. *See also* direct object. An objective element can also include indirect objects or the objects of prepositions.	1A	6
Order of Analysis: The order in which sentences are analyzed: phrases, clauses, principal elements, and modifiers.	1B	3
Ordinal Adjective: A word that denotes what place an object is in an order, such as *first, second, third*, or *fourth*.	1A	5
P		
Person: A property of a noun or pronoun that distinguishes among speaker, addressee, and others. There are three persons: first person (the one speaking), second person (the one being spoken to); and third person (the one being spoken about).	1A	7
Personal Pronoun: A pronoun that primarily takes the place of names of persons, hence *person*al pronoun. However, it can replace things too. *See also* pronoun, object pronoun, subject pronoun.	1A	7
Phrase: A group of words behaving like one part of speech. A phrase does not contain a subject and a predicate.	1A	3
Plural: A grammatical category for nouns, pronouns, and verbs that refer to more than one thing.	1A	3
Predicate: One of the principal elements in a sentence. It tells something about the subject like what it is doing or being.	1A	2
Predicate Verb: An action verb showing what the subject does.	1A	3

	Book & Level	Chapter
Preposition: A preposition is a part of speech used to show the relationship between certain words in a sentence. It is a word that joins its object, which is the noun or pronoun that follows it, to another word in a sentence, which can be a noun, pronoun, verb, adverb, or adjective. *WOL Level 1* focuses on prepositions that connect a noun or pronoun to a verb, showing a relationship of location (*where*), time (*when*), or manner (*how*). Some of the most common prepositions are *aboard, about, above, across, after, against, along, among, around, before, behind, below, beneath, beside, between, beyond, at, by, down, during, except, for, from, inside, in, into, near, of, off, on, out, outside, over, past, since, through, throughout, to, toward, under, up, until, upon, with, within, without, underneath.*	1B	3
Prepositional Phrase: A group of words including a preposition, an object of the preposition, and any words that modify that object. All these words together behave as a single part of speech, either an adverb or an adjective.	1B	3
Principal Clause: A group of words containing a subject and a predicate and able to stand independently as a sentence.	1A	4
Principal Elements: Principal elements are the parts of the sentence that are needed for the sentence to be completed. Subject and predicate are those parts.	1A	2
Pronoun: A pronoun is a part of speech used in place of a noun or of more than one noun. A pronoun is a part of speech.	1A	7
Proper noun: A noun that refers to a particular person, place, thing, or idea. It begins with a capital letter. *See also* common noun; noun.	1B	3

S

Second Person: A grammatical category for pronouns used by the speaker to refer to the person being spoken *to* (i.e., *you* as either a singular or plural subject pronoun or a singular or plural object pronoun). *See also* person.	1A	7

	Book & Level	Chapter
Sentence: A sentence is a group of words expressing a complete thought. There are four kinds of them: Declarative Sentence – Makes a statement. Interrogative Sentence – Asks a question. Imperative Sentence – Gives a command. Exclamatory Sentence – Expresses strong feeling.	1A	1
Simple Predicate: The verb or verb phrase in a sentence.	1A	3
Singular: A grammatical category for nouns, pronouns, and verbs that refer to only one thing.	1A	3
Stanza: A group of lines in a poem.	1A	3
Subject: One of the principal elements in a sentence. It is a noun or pronoun and is what the sentence is about.	1A	1
Subject Pronoun: A personal pronoun that is used as the subject in a sentence (i.e., *I, we, you, he, she, it, they*).	1A	7
Subject-Verb Agreement: A correct sentence structure in which the subject and verb agree in person (first, second, or third person) and number (singular or plural).	1B	2
Subordinate element: A word (or a group of words) that change or limit the meaning of the principal elements. Also known as a modifier.	1A	4
Synonym: A synonyms is a word that means almost the same thing as another word. For example, *happy* and *glad* are synonyms.	1B	6
Syntax: Word order. It is the way in which words are combined to form phrases, clauses, or sentences.	1A	2

T

Tense: A form of a verb that is used to show time or when an action occurs, as in past, present, and future.	1A	3
Third Person: A grammatical category for pronouns used by the speaker to refer to anyone or anything being spoken about that is not the speaker or the one addressed (i.e., the subject pronouns *he, she, it,* or *they* and the object pronouns *him, her,* or *them*). *See also* person.	1A	7

	Book & Level	Chapter
Transitive Verb: A verb that takes an objective element (i.e., a direct object). It transitions from the subject to the direct object.	1A	6

V

Verb: A part of speech that shows action or a state of being.	1A	3
Verb Phrase: A helping verb together with either an action verb or a linking verb.	1A	3
Vowel: A letter of the alphabet that represents a voiced speech sound. The indefinite article "an" is used before words beginning with vowels: *a, e, i, o, u*.	1A	5

Song Lyrics

Eight Parts of Speech *(1–1)*

The eight parts of speech are classes of words
with the same kind of meaning and use.
They are: nouns, verbs, adjectives, adverbs,
prepositions, pronouns, conjunctions, interjections.
These are the eight parts of speech,
classes of words with the same kind of meaning and use. *(Repeat.)*

Sentence *(1–2)*

A sentence is a group of words expressing a complete thought.
There are four kinds of sentences:
Declarative sentence—makes a statement.
Interrogative sentence—asks a question.
Imperative sentence—gives a command.
Exclamatory sentence—expresses strong feelings.
A sentence is a group of words expressing a complete thought.
There are four kinds of sentences. *(Repeat.)*

Principal Elements *(1–3)*

Principal elements are the parts of the sentence
that are needed for the sentence to be completed.
Subject and predicate are those two parts.

Subject and Predicate *(1–4)*

A subject, a subject is a noun or a pronoun
and is what the sentence is about *(clap, clap)*.
A predicate, a predicate tells us something about the subject
like what it is doing or being *(clap, clap)*.

From the Sideline: We recommend that you familiarize yourself with the songs and chants in the book before teaching them to your students.

When you see *(Repeat.)* at the end of a song, it means that all of the song lyrics are sung through once and then repeated. If *(repeat)* appears at the end of one or more lines in the song it means that those specific lines are repeated. For songs that have the notation *(echo)*, at the end of a line, you may want to split your class into two groups and have one group echo the other group as they sing the song.

Noun *(1–5)*

A noun is a part of speech.
It names a person, place, or thing.
A noun names a quality or an idea.
A noun is a part of speech.
It names a person, place, or thing.
A noun may be singular *(clap)* or plural *(clap clap clap)*. *(Repeat.)*

Verb and Helping Verb *(1–6)*

A verb is a part of speech. *(echo)*
A verb shows action or a state of being. *(echo)*
A verb is a part of speech. *(echo)*
A verb shows action or a state of being. *(echo)*
A helping verb helps another verb to express its meaning.
A helping verb stands near the verb.
It is called an auxiliary.
Am, is, are, was, were, be, being, been, has, have, had, do, does,
did, may, might, must, should, could, would, shall, will, *and* can.
A helping verb stands near the verb and is called an auxiliary.
A helping verb stands near the verb. It is called an auxiliary.

Adverb *(1–7)*

An adverb is a part of speech.
It modifies a verb or another adverb.
It can also modify an adjective
and answers three questions: *how? when*? or *where*?
It answers three questions: *how? when*? or *where*?

Adjective *(1–8)*

An adjective is a part of speech
used to describe or define
the meaning of a noun or pronoun.
It answers the questions:
How many? (echo)
Whose? (echo)
Which one? (echo)

or *What kind? (echo)*
It modifies a noun or pronoun.
It modifies a noun or pronoun.

Direct Object *(1–9)*

d-o, d-o
A direct object is an objective element
that tells what the subject is acting on.
d-o, d-o
It's a noun or pronoun after a transitive verb.
d-o, d-o
It answers the question *what* or *whom* after the verb
and is labeled *do*.

Four Classes of Verbs *(1–10)*

These are the four classes of verbs:
The four classes of verbs are transitive verbs, linking verbs,
intransitive verbs, and helping verbs.
These are the four classes of verbs.
A transitive verb takes an objective element.
A linking verb joins a subject to a predicate.
An intransitive verb does not take an objective element
or join a subject to a predicate.
A helping verb helps another verb express its meaning.
A helping verb helps another verb express its meaning.
These are the four classes of verbs.
These are the four classes of verbs.

Pronoun *(1–11)*

A pronoun is a part of speech
used in place of a noun or nouns.
A pronoun is a part of speech
used in place of a noun or nouns.
A pronoun is a part of speech.

Subject Pronouns *(1–12)*

Subject pronouns are in the nominative case:
I, you, he, she, it, we, you, they *(repeat)*.
Subject pronouns are in the nominative case:
I, you, he, she, it, we, you, they *(repeat)*.

Antecedent *(1–13)*

The antecedent is a noun, clause, or phrase
to which a pronoun refers.
If the antecedent is singular,
then the pronoun is singular too.
But if the noun, clause, or phrase is plural,
then the pronoun must be plural too.
The antecedent determines which pronoun is used.

Fable *(1–14)*

A fable (echo)
is a moral tale.
A fable (echo)
is not a fairy tale.
A fable is short, direct, and clear.
Animals are characters sneaky or sincere.
Teaching lessons not to be deceived,
fables warn us not to be naive.

Object Pronouns *(1–15)*

Object pronouns are in the objective case.
Me, you, him, her, it, us, you, them
Me, you, him, her, it, us, you, them.
Object pronouns are in the objective case.
Me, you, him, her, it, us, you, them
Me, you, him, her, it, us, you, them
Me, you, him, her, it, us, you, them.

Preposition *(1–16)*

A preposition *(a preposition)*
is a part of speech *(is a part of speech)*
used to show the relationship
between certain words in a sentence *(in a sentence)*. *(Repeat.)*

List of Prepositions *(1–17)*

Aboard, about, above, across, after, against, along, among, around
Preposition Words
Before, behind, below, beneath, beside, between, beyond, at, by
Preposition Words
Down, during, except, for, from, inside, in, into, near
Preposition Words
Of, off, on, out, outside, over, past, since, through
Preposition Words
Throughout, to, toward,
Under, up, until,
Upon, with, within,
Without, underneath
Preposition Words
Preposition Words
Preposition Words!

Phrase *(1–18)*

A phrase is a group of words
behaving like one part of speech
not containing a subject or a predicate. *(Repeat.)*

Object of the Preposition *(1–19)*

The object of the preposition
The object of the preposition
is the noun or pronoun
after the preposition. *(Repeat.)*

Conjunction *(1–20)*

A conjunction is a part of speech.
It joins elements of the same rank or name.
When two or more words are joined this way,
they're called compounds. *(Repeat.)*

Synonyms, Antonyms, and Homonyms *(1–21)*

Synonyms, antonyms, and homonyms
Synonyms are words that mean almost the same thing.
Antonyms are words that have the opposite meaning.
Homonyms are words that sound the same, but have different meaning and sometimes spelling—words that sound the same, but do not mean the same thing.
Synonyms, antonyms, and homonyms
Synonyms: little and small
Antonyms: short and tall
Homonyms: threw the ball, walk through the mall
Synonyms, antonyms, and homonyms
Synonyms, antonyms, and homonyms.

About the Title

The title of this series was inspired by a passage in a small book by Josef Pieper titled *Abuse of Language—Abuse of Power*. In the book, Pieper writes,

> [T]he well-ordered human existence, including especially its social dimension, is essentially based on the well-ordered language employed. A well-ordered language here does not primarily mean its formal perfection, even though I agree . . . that every correctly placed comma is decisive. No, a language is well ordered when its words express reality with as little omission as possible.[1]

Language is the means by which we make sense of reality. It is the medium by which we perceive truth. Therefore, a well-ordered language—one that best represents reality with as little distortion as possible—would provide the best access to truth. Language education, then, should be focused on developing as complete and accurate an understanding of language as possible.

While the pursuit of truth through language involves careful thinking (logic) and eloquent expression (rhetoric), the youngest students must first acquire a solid foundation in the structure and function of the language itself (grammar). Mirroring the well-ordered nature of language, effective educators employ an approach to language instruction that is itself well-ordered, structured, and disciplined. Critics of a well-organized and disciplined approach often confuse its form with the disposition of those who employ it. The disciplined approach to language study can be employed through intimidation and aggression, but it can just as easily be administered with love and compassion. The disciplined approach—often mischaracterized as "drill-and-kill"—actually respects the humanity of the student because it acknowledges that children learn differently than mature adults do.

For children to feast upon the rich cuisine of that which is good, true, and beautiful, they should first be shown how to taste, savor, and digest what they encounter. Without proper instruction that will cultivate their taste, students may turn from the "feast" in disgust, reject further sustenance, and perhaps never return. By acquiring a well-ordered language, students will also acquire that taste for language that will lead them to the great feast that awaits. To impart this taste is to avoid one of the greatest errors of modern educational theory, which is the assumption that children can learn without first acquiring those tools of learning that we call the language arts.

1. Josef Pieper, *Abuse of Language—Abuse of Power* (San Francisco: Ignatius Press, 1992), p. 36.

Notes

Notes